A HISTORY OF FELL...

FMC

ALAN H. FAULKNER

THE SEVENTH BOOK IN A SERIES COVERING ALL ASPECTS OF BOATING ON INLAND WATERWAYS

Fellows Morton and Clayton
Copyright A. H. Faulkner 2010

All rights reserved

ISBN 978-0-905366-37-1

First published 1975 (48 pages)
First published by The Belmont Press in 2010 (Fully revised and enlarged to 120 pages)

Prepared for press by Robert Wilson Designs

Printed for and published by
THE BELMONT PRESS   020-8907 4700
29 Tenby Avenue   Harrow   HA3 8RU
FAX 020-8907 7354   info@the-belmont-press.co.uk

The Robert Wilson Series

These books are a valuable resource for those interested in the history of waterways carrying boats of bygone days

RW1	THE NUMBER ONES	Robert J. Wilson
RW2	FENLAND BARGE TRAFFIC	Alan H. Faulkner
RW3	THE GEORGE & THE MARY	Alan H. Faulkner
RW4	MERSEY AND WEAVER FLATS	Edward Paget-Tomlinson
RW5	KNOBSTICKS	Robert J. Wilson
RW6	BOATS AND BOATYARDS	Robert J. Wilson
RW7	FELLOWS MORTON AND CLAYTON	Alan H. Faulkner
RW8	LIFE AFLOAT	Robert J. Wilson
RW9	TANKERS OF KNOTTINGLEY	Robert J. Wilson
RW10	ROSES & CASTLES	Robert J. Wilson
RW11	EPILOGUE	Robert J. Wilson
RW12	CLAYTON'S OF OLDBURY	Alan H. Faulkner
RW13	TOO MANY BOATS	Robert J. Wilson
RW14	SEVERN & CANAL AND CADBURY	Alan H. Faulkner
RW15	BARLOWS	Alan H. Faulkner

Between 1910 and 1912 photographs were taken of many of FMC's steamers as they passed through Long Buckby. The photographer is believed to have been Thomas William Millner who was the Grand Junction Canal Company's Assistant Engineer for the Northern District. This picture shows VULCAN apparently under way with an impressive wash, but there is no bow wave. This is because the boat has been tied back to the head of a lock by a stern rope, a practice adopted to give a sharper picture as the photographic emulsions of those days were much slower than in later years. (The Waterways Archive, Gloucester)

CHAPTER ONE
THE FORERUNNERS

Fellows, Morton and Clayton Limited (FMC) was arguably the best-known name in canal carrying circles in this country for many years. The company operated a large fleet of boats, which traded extensively over much of the inland waterways system carrying a wide variety of cargoes. It modelled many of its operations on those of Pickfords, who were once notable canal carriers providing a nationwide carrying service and some of their traffics passed, indirectly, to FMC.

Pickfords were already important carriers by road between London and Manchester when, in December 1786, they started to use the inland waterways. Initially this was from Manchester to Shardlow on the Trent & Mersey Canal in Derbyshire, with road transport being used between Shardlow and London, as the canal route further south was incomplete. With the opening of the Coventry Canal in 1790 the transhipment point was moved to Coventry and in 1796, with the opening of the first stretch of the Grand Junction Canal, it became Blisworth in Northamptonshire. The Grand Junction's long Blisworth tunnel was eventually completed in March 1805 thus opening up a direct canal route through to London, removing the need for transhipment and enabling Pickfords canal traffic to build up substantially.

From the core Manchester and London route Pickfords developed services to other places such as Derby in 1801, Birmingham in 1803 and Leicester in 1814 to name but a few. Much of the firm's trade involved switching goods from one service to another and this demanded a high degree of organisation at busy centres such as a key one at Braunston in Northamptonshire, where the Grand Junction joined the Oxford Canal, and an efficient clerical back-up to handle the paperwork.

Joshua Fellows (3 April 1834 – 23 April 1900) served as an FMC director from 27 September 1889 to 30 March 1900 and FMC's boats were often referred to as "Joshers" in affectionate memory of him. (Sandwell Community History & Archives Service)

Meanwhile a series of depots was established throughout the country where collection and delivery services were provided.

What was to become the firm's main base in London was established in 1820 at the City Road Basin, Islington on the Regent's Canal where a wharf and extensive warehousing facilities were set up. At the time the firm was operating over 80 narrow boats but the fleet reached its peak in 1838 with 116 craft and 398 horses.

From the late 1830s Pickfords began to switch part of their traffic to the railways and as that network expanded canal routes were progressively given up. Eventually the railway companies forced the firm to give up its entire long-distance canal carrying as a condition of if it retaining its railway agencies. As a result Pickfords relinquished its remaining canal carrying trade from 31 December 1847, only keeping a fleet of boats providing short-haul transhipment services between depots, factories and what became a large number of railway basins on the Birmingham Canal Navigations.

Alarmed at the potential loss of what was still a very significant amount of canal traffic, the Grand Junction Canal Company, which had been debating for some time whether to set up its own carrying operation, decided on 9 November 1847 finally to go ahead. A general manager had been appointed some months beforehand and he now opened negotiations not only to take over Pickfords canal traffic but also to acquire other carriers. In December the boats and business of German Wheatcroft & Son of Cromford were acquired. It had an important base at Paddington and ran extensive services to Birmingham, Manchester, Liverpool, Leicester, Nottingham, Burton-on-Trent, Derby, Cromford and down the river Trent to Newark and Gainsborough.

Soon after many of Pickfords remaining canal craft were purchased with the Grand Junction paying £2,800 and managing to retain much of the traffic. By the end of March 1848 the Grand

Thomas Clayton (30 July 1857 – 8 January 1927) served as an FMC director from 27 September 1889 to 28 September 1900. He married Sarah (née Blyth) on 13 November 1878 – she died on 5 March 1922. (Cath Turpin & Mrs Celia Harris)

Junction Canal Company's Carrying Establishment had 205 boats in service which had carried 2,248 tons over 43,260 miles in that month earning £3,059 in revenue against costs of £2,839.

A series of acquisitions followed including firms such as James & William Soresby of Cavendish Bridge, Shardlow, Worster & Company of Long Buckby, Crowley Hicklin & Company of Wolverhampton, Joseph Corbett & Sons of Stourbridge and John Whitehouse & Sons of Dudley. With these purchases the Carrying Establishment built up a chain of depots and agencies throughout much of the country, all controlled from its main base at the City Road Basin. At the same time a boat-building and repair yard was set up, initially at Paddington Basin but from February 1850 at Wenlock Basin, close to the City Road Basin, where a steady stream of boats were produced to modernise and expand the fleet.

The new boats were mostly named after districts around London, and particularly those bordering onto the river Thames, or after towns and villages throughout the rest of the country. On 28 January 1860 130 narrow boats were recorded for the company at the Watermen's Hall with names such as BLACKWALL, DEPTFORD, CARLISLE and SHEFFIELD. The company also had several barges, named mainly after rivers, operating on the river Thames. The new arrivals enabled some of the older boats to be sold with the first batch going in July 1850.

Despite its initial success the Carrying Establishment soon started trading at a loss and from the early 1850s a series of measures were introduced to redress the situation. In April 1855 these included transferring 13,000 tons of heavy iron castings traffic from Birmingham to London to The Trustees of the late James Fellows based at Tipton and to Price & Sons of Brierley Hill. Just under a year later the cheese and pottery trade from Cheshire and Stoke-on-Trent to London together with 18 boats was passed over to Mellor Colsell & Company.

Frederick Morton (10 January 1835 – 12 May 1921) served as an FMC Director from 27 September 1889 to 30 December 1920. (The Waterways Archive, Gloucester)

The company's letter heading taken from a letter sent by Henry Rodolph de Salis writing from Cornwall in May 1918 to Mr. Ironmonger. (Author's collection)

The Carrying Establishment was always progressive in its outlook and in 1860 experimented with mechanical propulsion by fitting up one if its boats with a steam engine and screw propeller. Named PIONEER, the boat performed well and in December 1860 the company ordered nine steamers, three with iron-hulls, three with wooden hulls and three with wooden hulls and iron sheets at the stern, all for its long-distance services, together with two large iron tugs for towing in the London area. They proved successful and further orders followed with the steamers being given names such as ANT, BEE and WASP.

Despite their success the carrying operations were still producing a loss and further economies had to be instituted such as giving up the Manchester traffic in 1865 and closing down some of the depots.

The Carrying Establishment's affairs took a dramatic turn for the worse on 2 October 1874 when three pairs of its boats, including the steamer READY, were on their way from the City Road Basin to Nottingham. As they were passing under the Macclesfield Bridge in Regent's Park TILBURY, one of the towed boats that was carrying a mixed cargo which included barrels of petroleum and barrels of gunpowder, exploded killing her crew of three instantaneously. The DEE alongside was badly damaged, LIMEHOUSE being towed behind was sunk, the bridge was destroyed and canal side properties were badly damaged. The Grand Junction had to pay out an enormous sum in compensation and coming on top of the trading losses this sealed the fate of the

Whilst not all the photographs of FMC steamers in the 1910 series have been found, those that exist provide a fine record of boats such as VICTORIA & ROUMANIA as shown here. (Laurence Hogg)

carrying operations, which were given up on 30 June 1876.

Most of the trade, however, was taken over by other carriers including two formed specifically for the purpose on 1 July 1876. One was the London & Staffordshire Carrying Company whose partners were Joshua Fellows of Tipton, his brother James, Hugh Hughes of Brentford and William Holcroft of Brierley Hill. Joshua Fellows was the managing partner in The Trustees of the late James Fellows whilst William Holcroft was the managing partner in Price & Sons, both of which had been involved in the 1855 take-over of the iron castings traffic. Hugh Hughes had been appointed

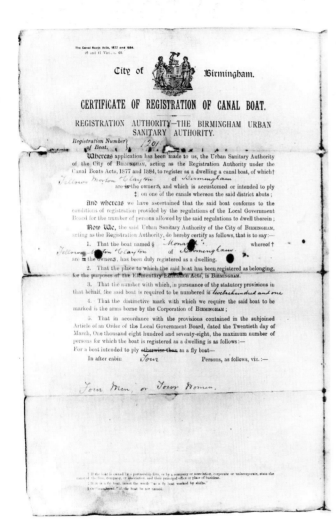

The public health registration certificate for the steamer MONARCH. The boat was inspected on 25 April 1908 and registered as a fly boat as Birmingham 1201 on 22 May 1908 to accommodate four adults. (Mrs Ada Gopsill)

traffic manager and general superintendent of the Carrying Establishment on 1 May 1868 and was already trading with some boats hired from the company. He went on to join Holcroft as a partner in Price & Sons.

The London & Staffordshire concentrated on business between London and Brentford and Birmingham, Wolverhampton and Stourbridge. Initially the firm had bases at Great Charles Street in Birmingham, Round Oak at Brierley Hill, Albion Wharf at Wolverhampton, and Stafford Wharf at Brentford with offices at Tipton. In December 1876 the partners leased a wharf in the City Road Basin from the Regent's Canal Company, guaranteeing a minimum of £150 in tolls each year but they gave this up two years later. Another early move was to establish a base at the Grand Junction Wharf at Ealing.

Some of the new firm's boats and several steamers were hired from the Carrying Establishment and in August 1877 the partners agreed to purchase these for £2,352 with payment being spread over 2½ years. In 1877 the Watermen's Hall records showed the firm as having the steamers FIDGET, HAVOC, NETTLE, PIONEER, READY and SWINGER, the steam tugs SHAMROCK and THISTLE, and 46 narrow boats several of which came from the GJCCCE such as BRIGHTON and PECKHAM.

The other new firm in 1876 was the London and Midland Counties Carrying Company which was set up by a group of the Grand Junction's agents to trade between the City Road Basin, Leicester, Nottingham and Derby. The partners took over at least a dozen of the Carrying Establishment's craft with Henry Watts, the leading partner, sending in a payment of £709 in October 1876 to cover the first two instalments. Subsequently the leases of the wharves at the City Road Basin and at Leicester and Nottingham were passed over to them. Frederick Cantrill was the partner in charge at Derby, a Mr. Hudson was based at Leicester and Alfred

FELLOWS, MORTON, & CLAYTON, Ltd.,
CANAL CARRIERS

WHARVES

on the

REGENT'S CANAL,

30, Wharf Road,
City Road.

✳ ✳

Telephone :

NORTH 565.

WHARVES

on the

Grand Junction Canal,

Brentford.

✳ ✳

Telephone :

EALING 49.

BY STEAM BOATS

To the Midland Counties, Birmingham, South Staffordshire, and the North.

APPLY FOR RATES AND INFORMATION AS ABOVE, OR TO THE CITY OFFICE—

4, CATHERINE COURT, SEETHING LANE, E.C.   TELEPHONE: AVENUE 987.

And at LIVERPOOL, MANCHESTER, NOTTINGHAM, NORTHAMPTON, LEICESTER, &c.

Registered Office : BIRMINGHAM.   Telephone Nos. : Central 532 and 533.

An advertisement for the company that appeared in the Regent's Canal & Dock Company's booklet that was published in July 1911. (Regent's Canal & Dock Company Booklet)

Landon managed the important base at 30 Wharf, City Road, which the firm took over from the Grand Junction.

Despite the sales to these two new carriers and to others the Carrying Establishment was left with many surplus craft and on 3 October 1876 an auction was held at Fazeley Street in Birmingham and a week later at the City Road Basin to dispose of them. These sales included 34 narrow boats, 3 barges, 7 steamers, 12 steam tugs and other craft. Following this the boatyard at Wenlock Basin was closed down leaving the Grand Junction to write off its carrying losses to experience.

The founding father of FMC was James Fellows, who was born on 6 March 1805 at Sedgley to Joshua and Nancy Fellows. On 2 June 1828 he married Eliza Hyde at All Saints Church, West Bromwich and they had twelve children, the first, Eliza being born

Harry Beresford stands in the stern of BUCKINGHAM, with the steamer PHOENIX behind, whilst the pair were passing through Lock No 9 at Long Buckby (The Waterways Archive, Gloucester)

The steamers VICTORIA and EMPEROR and a cluster of other boats moored above the Gauging Locks at Brentford. (Walter Russon)

on 20 February 1811 at Gornal. Their second daughter, Mary, was born in April 1831 and baptised at the Upper Gornal Independent Church in April 1834 when her father was described as a miner living at Upper Gornal. She was baptised for the second time in June 1836, on this occasion at All Saints Church, Sedgley, when her father was now described as a canal carrier's agent living at Coseley.

In 1837 James Fellows became a canal carrier in his own right based at West Bromwich. On 1 January 1839 he was granted toll credit by the Warwick & Napton Canal Company meaning that his boats did not have to pay the canal tolls in cash at the toll station but could enjoy the benefits of a monthly or quarterly account. Likewise on 30 January 1839 his boat PROVIDENCE was weighed for toll assessment purposes at Braunston by the Grand Junction Canal Company prior to it trading down to London and a series of other boats followed on and are recorded in that company's registers.

By 1841 James had moved to Lockside at Tipton and in 1845, or soon after, he moved into Horseley House at Toll End, Tipton. Officially he described himself as a "Canal and Railway Carrier" but it would appear his railway involvement was on a small scale and possibly in the nature of a forwarding agency. James died on 17 May 1854, aged 49 years.

Meanwhile on 3 April 1834 Joshua Fellows was born at Sedgley, the eldest son of James and Eliza Fellows, and he went on to follow in his father's footsteps. Like his sister Mary, Joshua was baptised twice - at the Upper Gornal Independent Church on 13 July 1834 and then at All Saints Church, Sedgley on 26 June 1836. At an early age he entered his father's business but when James died he was still under age, which prevented him from becoming a partner. Initially James's widow Eliza together with Thomas Bagnall, who had been involved with James in the business for several years, carried on trading as "The Trustees of the late James Fellows" with the profits being divided equally between them.

Joshua was employed in the business on a salary of £80 but as soon as he reached the age of twenty-one he was admitted as an equal partner with his mother and Bagnall - in his first year to 31 March 1856 he received £934 as his share of the profits. Thomas Bagnall left the business from 30 September 1857 with his share

EARL & WARWICK underway at Long Buckby in 1910. (D.L. McDougall)

of the profits then passing to Eliza Fellows.

In addition to sharing in the profits the partners received an allowance of £26 per annum for each boat used by the firm, as the individual partners owned all these. On 30 September 1854 Eliza had 18 boats and Joshua 4; three years later the numbers had risen to 23 and 13 respectively and by the end of 1867 to 56 and 28. In that year Joshua received £709 as his share of the profits and his mother £1,419. In the meantime but probably in 1859 a boat-building yard had been established beside the Toll End Communication Canal just north of Workhouse Lane Bridge on land owned by Eliza.

On 8 April 1857 Joshua Fellows married Mary Haines at St. Mary's Church, Tipton. She had been born in 1835 at Tipton to Job Haines, an iron master, and his wife Mary. Initially Joshua and his wife lived at Market Place, Wednesbury but in about 1865 they

moved to Churchfield House, West Bromwich. They had at least ten children, the eldest being Frederick William who was born in 1860 and followed his father into the family's canal carrying business. At least two other brothers were later involved with FMC - John Arthur, who became a gun stock merchant living at Barnt Green, being a shareholder whilst Frank Eagleton ultimately became a director.

Not content with simply increasing the size of their fleet the Fellows expanded the scope of their operations and Joshua played a leading role in this. In July 1861 a branch was established at Shardlow, on the Trent & Mersey Canal, with the two partners each investing £1,000 in the new venture. It contributed a modest £200 trading profit in its first year and this had risen to £450 by 1867. In May 1863 mother and son each invested £1,200 in the business of Rogers & Company, which was based at Brentford at

14

Steamer EMPRESS with her butty WALES in one of the Gas Two Locks (Nos 51 & 52) at Berkhamsted. (Black Country Museum)

the southern end of the Grand Junction Canal. The firm's growing trade to London was reflected in 47 boats being registered at the Watermen's Hall in London on 8 June 1863 for Eliza, Joshua and a Charles Davies who probably managed the newly acquired Brentford business from Stafford Wharf. Soon after several sailing barges and open barges were acquired indicating the firm was trading out onto the river Thames.

Another significant move came from the 1 January 1865 when "J. Fellows & Company" was established at Gloucester with the two partners each investing £1,000. In 1870 the small carrying

businesses operated by both the Staffordshire & Worcestershire Canal Company and by the Worcester & Birmingham Canal Company were acquired. The former had been started in 1847 and in 1851 had taken over the business of William Partridge who traded between Birmingham and Gloucester. It also operated tugs on the river Severn. Meanwhile the Worcester & Birmingham's business had been started in 1848 and had probably taken over some of the trade of John Danks, a carrier between Birmingham and Worcester.

Even before these acquisitions the Fellows had built up a fair-

sized business based at Gloucester - by 31 December 1869 they owned the steamer EDMUND IRONSIDES which traded between Gloucester and Cork in Southern Ireland, the Bristol trows ALMA and UNITY, barges SARAH and TRUE BLUE and 21 canal boats such as BATH and BROMSGROVE, 14 sets of cloths, 19 horses and 9 mules, all valued at £2,800, and the business had accumulated profits of £2,900 on top of the original capital of £2,000.

In 1873 the business of "J Fellows & Co." based at Gloucester was merged in with that of rival carriers Danks and Sanders into a new limited liability company - The Severn and Canal Carrying, Shipping and Steam Towing Company Limited. The management was then shared between Joshua Fellows, his brother James based at Worcester Wharf in Birmingham and Joseph Danks based at Stourport with agents at places like Worcester and Gloucester. The new company had an extensive trade not only on the river Severn and the canals connecting with the Midlands but also out in to the Bristol Channel to South Wales and Ireland.

Another area where Joshua became involved was at Wolverhampton, trading to the Potteries and the north-west. The first sections of the Trent & Mersey Canal to be opened were at its eastern end and by June 1770 the line from the river Trent at Derwent Mouth through Shardlow and Burton-on-Trent to Shugborough and Great Haywood, where it joined the Staffordshire & Worcestershire Canal, was open. Shortly afterwards Hugh Henshall, with the involvement of a group of the canal's shareholders, established a carrying company – "Hugh Henshall & Company" – to develop trade on the canal between Shardlow and Great Haywood. Henshall was already closely involved with the building of the canal and he took over as its engineer on the death of his brother-in-law, James Brindley, in September 1772.

The Trent & Mersey extended westwards to Stone in November 1771, to Stoke-on-Trent in October 1772, through the

The engine from the steamer ADMIRAL was a vertical tandem compound designed by William Howard Haines and manufactured under licence by FMC. (The Waterways Archive, Gloucester)

16

long Harecastle tunnel to Sandbach in April 1775 and finally to the Bridgewater Canal at Preston Brook in May 1777 and the Henshall carrying business expanded with it. Its initial bases were at Shardlow and Stoke with its own boatyard at Shardlow where both wide beam craft for operation on the river Trent and narrow boats were built. Most of the wide-beam craft appear to have been sold off to the Gainsborough Boat Company in the late 1790s but the company remained as an important narrow boat carrier being taken over by the Trent & Mersey at about the same time and operating as a wholly owned subsidiary. Apart from trade on its own canal the firm developed services to Wolverhampton and Birmingham.

Henshalls had always had close relations with the Duke of Bridgewater and from an early date had rented one of his large warehouses at Castlefield, Manchester. Following the duke's death in 1803 these good relations continued with his trustees but in 1846 the North Staffordshire Railway Company purchased the Trent & Mersey. The deal included the Henshall carrying subsidiary, which still was conducting some trade to and from the West Midlands, based on Wolverhampton.

Meanwhile Maurice and James Shipton, who were originally timber merchants at Birmingham, had established a branch of their business at Albion Wharf, Horseley Fields, Wolverhampton in 1821 and had gone on to develop an extensive canal carrying trade. In 1847 the North Staffordshire Railway acquired that part of Shiptons' business that was based at Wolverhampton and appointed George Skey, James Shipton's son in law, as its agent there.

Alarmed by so much of Henshalls and Shiptons former carrying trade falling into railway hands, the Bridgewater Trustees began sending their own boats down into South Staffordshire providing strong competition to the North Staffordshire Railway whose

The boiler from the steamer ADMIRAL was built by John Thompson & Co. Ltd of Wolverhampton in 1905 for £70. It had 44 tubes (2¼-inch diameter) and 10 stay tubes with a working pressure of 110 pounds per square inch. (The Waterways Archive, Gloucester)

The steamer EMPRESS and her butty leaving Batchworth Lock No 81 on the Grand Junction Canal at Rickmansworth on their way south. The lock on the left led up to a small basin and to Rickmansworth Town Wharf. (T. W. King Collection)

trade was seriously undermined. This prompted an agreement dated 29 September 1849 whereby the Trustees purchased the North Staffordshire's Wolverhampton-based canal carrying operations, which also extended to Birmingham, Dudley, Walsall and the surrounding district. James Shipton was appointed as the Trustees' agent and under a separate agreement dated 23 October 1849 Shipton & Company were appointed agents and were required to provide up to 35 boats for the Trustees' traffic between the Midlands and Preston Brook, to provide a collection and delivery service in the Midlands, and to carry the Trustees' traffic to and from London as required. Shiptons finally withdrew from the London service in the middle of 1853 due to strong railway competition.

The Trustees already operated extensive services based on the Bridgewater Canal and the river Mersey and they went on to consolidate their position in the South Staffordshire area. In July 1850 the Fellows were appointed as agents followed by Price &

Sons of Brierley Hill in October 1851 and Joseph Whitehouse of West Bromwich in March 1856. Further afield Daniel Brown of Nottingham was appointed in December 1853 and there were others such as at Derby. By 1869 the trustees' agent at Wolverhampton was Frederick Morton.

Morton had been born on 10 January 1835 at Hinckley in Leicestershire, the son of Daniel and Hannah Morton, and was baptised there on 6 February. In 1858 he entered the canal carrying business and it almost certain this was as an employee of the Bridgewater Trustees. On 17 December 1861 he married Mary Haylings at Eccles Parish Church being described as a cashier living at Tranmere near Birkenhead. Mary had been born in 1839 at Malvern in Worcestershire. Their first child, Frederick George, was born in 1863 in Dublin where it is believed Morton was working for the Bridgewater Trustees at their office in that city. He soon moved back to England as his second son, John William, was born in September 1864 at Barton on Irwell, his father being

A group of FMC boat people outside the Six Bells Inn at Brentford in 1905. Left to right: Jack Gill (captain of steamer SULTAN); George Jones (mate of steamer COLONEL); Jacob Whitehouse (SULTAN's mate); Mrs Hannah Bevington (MIDDLESEX's mate); Thomas Edwin Bevington (MIDDLESEX's captain) and Thomas Walker (SULTAN's driver). (Mrs M. E. Russon)

recorded as agent for the Trustees. His third son, Harold, was born in 1868 or 1869 at Wolverhampton.

By 1873 the Fellows had established a base at Railway Street in Wolverhampton and appointed Frederick Morton as their agent. However he maintained his connection with the Bridgewater Trustees and with what became the Bridgewater Navigation Company Limited in 1872 and this led to the reconstitution of the Trustees of the Late James Fellows into a new partnership - "Fellows Morton and Company" - from 1 July 1876. The formation of the Bridgewater Navigation Co. Ltd. was undoubtedly a factor in this new venture but it was also prompted by the death of Eliza Fellows on 20 September 1875 aged 64 years as she still had a major financial interest in the family business.

The partners of the new firm were Joshua Fellows of West Bromwich, his brother James Fellows of Edgbaston and Frederick Morton of Wolverhampton. The business traded as railway and canal carriers and forwarding agents, its main traffics being between Birmingham, Wolverhampton and Liverpool and it had bases at Great Charles Street in Birmingham, Albion Wharf in Wolverhampton and Horseley in Tipton. James Fellows withdrew from the partnership in 1884 to concentrate on his other interests.

As part of the new arrangements Fellows Morton entered into an agreement to take over all the trade between South Staffordshire, Preston Brook, Runcorn, Ellesmere Port, Manchester and Liverpool previously handled by the Bridgewater Navigation Co. Ltd. The agreement, which was signed on 19 September 1876 but was effective from 1 July, was for an initial five-year term and involved Fellows Morton taking over 34 boats valued at £2,374 together with horses and some wagons. The partners were allowed to purchase the boats over 2½ years but the horses, wagons, vans and other equipment acquired had to be paid for up front. The use of rented property included a wharf

With the steamer EMPEROR in the foreground, the steamer QUEEN behind and another unidentified steamer at the back, this cluster of FMC boats wait for a stoppage to clear at Long Buckby. (The Waterways Archive, Gloucester)

The steamer PHOENIX being gauged at Long Buckby Lock No 9. (The Waterways Archive, Gloucester)

in Birmingham, offices in both Birmingham and Wolverhampton, and stables at Wolverhampton and Audlem.

Fellows Morton went on to become a major carrier and soon expanded into other areas, the first acquisition being part of the London & Staffordshire Carrying Company's business. In March 1877 a section of the Grand Junction's wharf at Fazeley Street in Birmingham had been leased to John Griffiths at £90 per annum, but two months later the London & Staffordshire agreed to take over part of Griffiths' trade and also the tenancy of the wharf. Their occupation was also short-lived as in October 1878 they gave

notice to quit from 25 March 1879, the same day as they also gave up their premises at Brentford. Joshua Fellows stepped in and took over the Fazeley Street lease and this soon became Fellows Morton's main wharf for dealing with traffic from the Grand Junction and Warwick Canals. Soon after the London & Staffordshire's business was split with the major share being taken on by Fellows Morton and the remainder by William Holcroft at Brierley Hill.

Fellows Morton went on to lease additional premises from the Warwick & Birmingham Canal at Warwick Wharf, Fazeley Street

The steamer SULTAN tows the butty ASH through Syon Park, upstream from Brentford in September 1903. (William Knibbs)

and in 1883 the firm also leased premises further east on the canal which included stables and where, in 1886, a small boat-building yard was established. In the same year the carrying businesses of both William Beckett of Leicester and Daniel Brown of Nottingham, which included wharves in both cities, were acquired and land was leased from the Regent's Canal Company at its Limehouse dock and a small depot was established there, the partners having to guarantee 5,000 tons of traffic generating a minimum of £100 per annum in tolls.

The final acquisition came in November 1887, after a year of negotiations, when the London and Midland Counties Carrying Company was acquired. It operated from the City Road Basin and had wharves at Leicester, Nottingham and Derby but soon after the take-over the wharf at Derby was given up with an agent, John Gandy, being appointed instead and at about the same time Sidney Peters was appointed the firm's agent at Coventry. As part of the London & Midland Counties deal Fellows Morton negotiated toll reductions on traffic to and from the East Midlands with the Grand Junction agreeing a 25% rebate when the tolls exceeded £1,400 each year. In May 1888 the rebates for

the previous year amounted to £304 for through traffic and £24 for local trade.

Another area where Fellows Morton was involved was on the river Trent and Humber. On 28 June 1882 the firm, in partnership with Richard Lee Furley of Furley & Company of Hull, entered into agency agreements with the Trent Navigation Company. The arrangement may not have been entirely satisfactory as Joshua Fellows slowly reduced his firm's involvement with Furley and withdrew altogether in 1886; despite this Furley & Co. remained as Fellows' Hull agents for many years.

The scene was now set for an even more important move.

CHAPTER TWO
COMPANY FORMATION

On 3 July 1889 Fellows, Morton and Clayton Limited was incorporated with the company number 29283 to take over the business of Fellows Morton & Company and part of the business of William Clayton of Saltley.

William Clayton had been born on 9 July 1818 at Yiewsley in Middlesex, the eldest son of William and Mary Ann Clayton. On 15

COLONEL & WATFORD were included in the Long Buckby 1910 series. (Author's Collection)

April 1839 he married Catherine Johnson at Hillingdon parish church, he being recorded as a boatman, and in 1842 he set up as a canal carrier in his own right based at West Drayton.

A narrow boat was gauged for him by the Grand Junction Canal Company on 4 October 1850 and another, named TRENT, followed on 10 November 1853 starting a tradition of giving most of the boats river names. In about 1845 the family moved to Aston in Birmingham and Clayton set up another base at Salford Bridge on the Birmingham & Fazeley Canal. He soon became well established in the Midlands and was handling a variety of general cargoes such as imported timber from London with paving stones from Rowley Regis and clay drain pipes often making up a return loading to London.

In April 1862 Clayton rented premises on the Birmingham & Warwick Junction Canal at Saltley and he then moved his base there, establishing Park Wharf and eventually setting up a small boatyard. By this time, however, he had started to deal in timber and to expand his canal business into the more specialised task of transporting liquids in his boats. Many gasworks had been

established throughout the country and their by-products included crude tar and gas water, a liquid rich in ammonia used for manufacturing fertilisers. By the end of 1863 Clayton was taking crude tar from the London area to Birmingham for distillation on a regular basis, many gasworks being purposely sited beside canals to enable them to be supplied with coal by boat. Initially the liquids were transported in barrels but ultimately the holds of the boats were adapted so that the liquid could be carried in bulk and simply pumped out at its destination.

The Birmingham and Staffordshire Gas Light Company had built a works at Adderley Street, Birmingham, on the Warwick & Birmingham Canal in 1844 and in 1858 it built another works at Saltley where Clayton was on hand to offer his services. Ten years later he was handling considerable tonnages of crude tar, gas-water and other by-products from both these works to destinations on the Birmingham Canal Navigations.

William and Catherine Clayton had ten children of whom their eldest son, William John, was born on 13 May 1844 at Hillingdon. He was originally a coal merchant but in the 1870s he took over his

An early picture of the steamer PRESIDENT but possibly not from the 1910 Long Buckby series. She entered service in 1909, was converted to a motor boat in 1925 and was sold by FMC in 1946. By 1953 she had become a maintenance boat and was offered for sale as a hulk in 1973. She was rescued and restored as a steamer by Malcolm Braine and Nicholas Bostock in 1978. (Richard Thomas)

Between 1910 and 1912 four wide boats - BRAUNSTON, HAREFIELD, ISLEWORTH and ISLINGTON - were built at the Uxbridge Dock to work up to places like Kings Langley Mill. They are pictured here at Brentford. All four were requisitioned during the First World War and used by the military on the French canals. (Birmingham Central Library)

father's timber business at Saltley, which he incorporated to become W. J. Clayton Limited. The links with his father's canal business were maintained, as it became the major carrier of the imported timber with much of it being transhipped from barges at Nottingham. To handle this traffic William Clayton had established a depot at Old Lenton on the Nottingham Canal where several boats were based including some barges that traded down the river Trent to Gainsborough.

Catherine Clayton died on 17 February 1873 aged 54 years and William went on to marry for the second time but this marriage did not last long as he died on 4 July 1882 at Saltley just before his 64th birthday, having built up his business into a thriving concern. His third son, Thomas, who had been born on 30 July 1857 at Bowyer Road, Saltley, and had been employed in his father's business for several years, now took over, albeit continuing to trade in his father's name.

Under Thomas the growth continued being helped by the opening of further gasworks. By 1885 tar was being collected for distillation in Birmingham from Solihull gasworks, established in

1869, from Leamington gasworks, first established in 1819, and from further afield such as Northampton. Meanwhile creosote was being taken from the Midlands to the river Thames at Brentford and on to the river Lee.

On 1 April 1896 an important contract was obtained to carry creosote to the Bulls Bridge depot of the Great Western Railway at Southall. The railway had established a sleeper depot beside the canal there and depended on barges to deliver the timber from the London docks and on Claytons to deliver the creosote that was used to preserve the wood.

During all this time Thomas Clayton had continued to build up the numbers of boats in his fleet. In January 1860 William Clayton had 16 canal boats recorded at the Watermen's Hall and others followed on over the next 22 years. In April 1883 and after Thomas's take over, 42 craft were recorded for the business and others followed on with several acquired from Joseph Whitehouse of West Bromwich such as BIRKENHEAD, LIVERPOOL, and RUNCORN, which had almost certainly originated in the Grand Junction's fleet. These craft were not renamed becoming

25

The wide boat PIONEER makes a slash as it is launched from the Uxbridge Dock in 1935. (Author's collection)

exceptions to the normal procedure of adopting river names. The acquisitions also included the steam boats PIRATE and SPEEDWELL, which were purchased from John Smedley of Birmingham and were used on the long-distance services between London, Birmingham and Nottingham. Thomas Clayton also established a link with Fellows Morton & Company who built the new steamer VICTORIA for him at their Tipton dock towards the end of 1888.

From this link came the idea of a merger between the two businesses but leaving out Claytons bulk liquid carrying side and it was to achieve this that the new limited company was set up.

FMC's Memorandum of Association, which gave the new company very wide-ranging powers, stated that the first object was

"To acquire the business of Messrs. Fellows and Morton and Mr. Thomas Clayton of Birmingham in the County of Warwick and elsewhere, and the freehold and leasehold property, trade and other contracts, agency agreements, stock-in-trade, chattels, horses, carts, wagons, carriages, boats, steamers, fixed and movable plant, goods, effects and things used therein...."

26

With the wide boat PIONEER safely launched, the Uxbridge dockyard staff pose for their photograph in 1935. (Walter Russon)

It went on to authorise the company to act as a carrier in Great Britain, Ireland and elsewhere and to convey all manner of people and goods by canal, railway, land or sea or in any other manner. The company was also to be able to act as contractors, engineers, boat builders, blacksmiths, straw and corn dealers, coal merchants, ship, barge and boat owners, ice manufacturers and a very wide range of other activities covering virtually every aspect ever likely to be encountered in its business.

On 12 June 1889 two agreements had been signed covering the take-over of the businesses. The first was between Joshua Fellows, Frederick Morton and Thomas Instone who acted as trustee for the new company and covered Fellows Morton & Company which was taken over effectively from 1 January 1889. It included the purchase of 8 steamers, some 84 unpowered narrow boats, 3 barges, horses, vans and carts, equipment, premises and goodwill all for £45,000.

A valuation had been carried out and the individual prices of some of the boats acquired have been traced. For instance CHINA and LUDLOW, both of which had been built at Tipton at about the same time that the new company was set up, were valued at £160 each, whereas WEAVER and WINDSOR, built there just over a year earlier, were worth £142 each. BILSTON, built at Tipton in the autumn of 1886, was valued at £80 but the older boats attracted a somewhat lower figure. COLE, which had to be renamed TEES to avoid duplication with a similarly named boat in Clayton's fleet, dated back to 1878 and was valued at £60, SHARDLOW dating back at least to 1874 was £52 and RUGBY was a mere £20.

The second agreement was between Thomas Clayton and Thomas Instone and covered the general carrying side of the business of William Clayton, which was taken over effectively from 1 June 1889. It included the acquisition of 3 steamers, 30 narrow boats, plant, equipment, the premises and boat dock at Saltley and goodwill all for £20,353. 5s. 9d.

Here again the individual prices of some of the boats acquired have been traced. ANKER, ARROW and COLE, which were built at Saltley in 1889 and hence were virtually new, were acquired for

£160 each representing their cost of construction. TIBER, built in 1888, was valued at £155, OHIO in 1887 was £130, STORT in 1886 £125, USK in 1883 £115, TAME in 1882 £105, SHANNON in 1881 £95, and NENE in 1874 £80.

Thomas Clayton retained those boats involved in the collection of liquids and he continued to run this business but now in his own name. As Park Wharf, Saltley was included in the transfer to FMC he had to find new premises and he relocated to land at Tat Bank, Oldbury that was convenient as it was close to the Springfield Tar Works, one of the main destinations for the cargoes of crude tar. On 5 September 1889 17 boats, comprising most of those not taken over by FMC, were recorded for him at the Watermen's Hall.

On 4 July1889, the day after FMC was incorporated, a prospectus was issued seeking subscribers for 7,500 ordinary shares of £10 each on which it was proposed to call up only £6 initially, and 2,500 6% cumulative preference shares of £10 each, a total of £100,000. Subscribers were required to pay £1 on application and £5 on allotment with the balance being called later. The total authorised capital was to be £120,000 in ordinary and £30,000 in preference shares. One reason FMC was set up was to attract additional monies into the business and hence enable it to expand.

The prospectus recorded that Powell and Brown, surveyors and valuers of Tipton had made a professional valuation, in January and May 1889 of the assets of the two businesses to be acquired and this amounted to £49,640. 4s. 6d. This figure included the freehold and leasehold premises at Birmingham, Brentford, City Road Basin, Leicester, Nottingham, Saltley, Tipton and Wolverhampton, plant and stock including the canal boats, steamers and barges, horses, vans, carts, and an ice-making machine at Leicester.

Joshua Fellows, Frederick Morton and Thomas Clayton were

The wide boat PIONEER on its trial run from the Uxbridge Dock (Birmingham Central Library)

to be appointed joint managing directors of FMC but they did not join the board until 27 September after the initial allotment of shares had been completed. The company's first chairman was Alderman Reuben Farley, a Justice of the Peace, Chairman of the Ironfounders Association and who lived at West Bromwich. He was related to Joshua Fellows as he had married Elizabeth Haines, the third daughter of Job and Mary Haines and sister of Joshua's wife Mary. The other directors were Major Alfred Ash, JP, who lived at The Mount, Washwood, and Major Henry Williams, JP, of Rockingham Hall, Hagley. Ash was married to Matilda Clayton, the second daughter of William and Catherine Clayton, and was thus brother-in-law to Thomas and it seems likely that Henry Williams was also related to one of the three managing directors.

The board met for the first time on 25 July at 83 Colmore Row, Birmingham, the offices of William Shakespeare, one of the two solicitors who had been acting in the company formation. Thereafter the meetings were held at Lower Fazeley Street usually on a monthly basis.

Even before FMC was formed the directors were planning their first takeover. It had been represented to them that a large traffic potential existed with the various towns and businesses on the river Thames between Oxford and London. As a result the prospectus announced that negotiations had been started with the Oxford and London Tug Co. Ltd. to purchase and develop the carrying business it had started on the river. The intention was for the tug company's directors then to take up shares in FMC and the initial shareholder's list indicates this took place.

In August the tug company was taken over and its steam barge WILD ROSE came into FMC's ownership together with premises at Folly Wharf in Oxford and a wharf at Reading. The venture seems not to have been very successful and probably did not last for long as the Oxford wharf was given up in about June 1892 and that at Reading soon after.

Another acquisition came in December 1889 when the long-distance part of the rival carrying business operated by John Fanshaw and John Foster Pinson from Commercial Road,

Accidents will happen – the butty STOCKPORT capsized in the Weigh Dock at Brentford in May 1910, necessitating the dock having to be drained to start the recovery process. (Author's Collection)

The experimental wide steamer SWAN pictured in 1911 at Brentford whilst on trial with Charles Newton at the tiller. She had an oil-fired steam engine, was 10½-feet wide and could carry 34 tons, but ultimately she proved a failure as she did not travel so well in the restricted channel of the canal. (Arthur Newton)

An early picture of LINDOLA, the first motor boat to be built at FMC's Uxbridge boatyard, with George Foss at the tiller. Her exhaust pipe was bent over to avoid blasting debris off the underside of bridges and tunnels. In April 1919 LINDOLA, along with QUAIL and RAVEN, which were all fitted up as single motors at the time, operated a service transporting workers and staff between Salford Bridge and the large Fort Dunlop factory at Aston Cross. (The Waterways Archive, Gloucester)

Wolverhampton, was acquired involving at least 13 boats. Meanwhile some barges had been acquired in November from Nash & Miller of Vicarage Wharf, Battersea for operation on the Thames.

Another venture for the new company was to develop a new canal basin and premises on the Warwick & Birmingham Canal some 200 yards east of the original Warwick Wharf and fronting onto Fazeley Street. Fellows Morton had first taken part of the wharf premises here in 1883 but in August 1889 plans had been produced for a major extension and a new basin to provide increased loading and unloading facilities. A year later work was well in hand and in September 1891 FMC was able to report the basin was complete, suitable wharf cranes had been erected, the yard had been roofed in and the warehousing area extended. Most of the land had originally been used for a gasworks by the Birmingham Gas Light & Coke Company but it had been closed down in 1878.

At the same time 3,000 square yards of land had been purchased at nearby Liverpool Street on which to build stabling to replace that it was having to use at Saltley, which was two miles from Fazeley Street where the bulk of the traffic was handled. The development was completed by the middle of 1892 with accommodation being provided for 83 horses with a blacksmith's shop, a saddler's shop and a house for a caretaker also being provided. In all FMC spent some £5,483 on this project.

FMC's first financial accounting period ran to 30 June 1890, the results being affected by a dock labourer's strike in London, which badly interrupted trade and caused a serious loss, and an epidemic of Russian influenza which resulted in many deaths amongst the company's horses. Despite this the company was able to report a profit of £5,430 permitting maiden dividends of 6% to be paid on both the ordinary and the preference shares. It was a promising

FMC's boats MARSWORTH & LANGLEY are believed to be have been the first loaded boats to use the Inclined Plane Boat Lift that was opened at Foxton on 11 July 1900. (The Waterways Archive, Gloucester).

start.

CHAPTER 3
THE STEAMERS

In the July 1889 share prospectus there was an important clause that dealt with the new company's steamers.

"The Vendors having expended a large amount in making and improving canal steamers (of which they have ten at work and another on the stocks) have succeeded in constructing them to carry larger cargoes than formerly with great saving in consumption of fuel. The Company are now in a position, and have the necessary premises and plant, to at once construct canal boats, steamers and engines, on the most perfect and approved plans to date. The steel boat and engineering establishment is at Fazeley Street, Birmingham, and the wood boat building and repairing yards at Tipton and Saltley."

The Fazeley Street yard had been set up by Fellows Morton in 1886 and had produced a series of boats constructed entirely of mild steel plates 3/16 inches thick The first was a horse boat named EUROPE and she was followed by ASIA, AFRICA, AMERICA and GANGES. They cost £218 each except for GANGES in 1889, which cost £230, these figures being considerably more than a comparable wooden boat at the time. In addition five steamers were built of the same material starting with EMPRESS in October 1887 at a cost of £600, PRINCESS in 1888 at £600 and DUCHESS and DUKE in March 1889 at £625 each. The steamer mentioned in the prospectus as being on the stocks was COUNTESS, which was completed in February 1890 at a cost of £650.

These early steel boats were not very successful in service and did little work before being rebuilt or sold. This was probably due to the abrasive conditions in which they worked and to corrosion,

SULTAN & KEGWORTH alongside FMC's Nottingham depot and warehouse. (Nottingham Historical Film Unit)

ENVOY & WALSALL together with several Trent river craft lie alongside the Trent Navigation Company's wharf and warehouse in Nottingham. (Birmingham Central Library)

for at the time the mild steels available were far less resistant than contemporary iron. Nonetheless steel had been used in ship building circles and Fellows Morton no doubt wanted to follow this lead. By using steel up to a ton could be saved in the overall weight of the boat and this would have meant increased cargo capacity.

The claim in the prospectus about greater carrying capacity however could have been for an altogether different reason. The steamer layout inherited from the Grand Junction was very compact and as beam and draught were fixed, the only way to increase capacity would have been to lengthen the hold. The boats themselves could not be made longer and it was unlikely the

engine room and cabin could have been made significantly shorter. Assuming the improvement became permanent it seems possible the early Grand Junction steamers had traditional hulls and Fellows Morton may have been responsible for introducing the counter stern.

The locks govern boat length and in a horse boat this is made up of the complete hull plus the overhang of the rudder when turned sideways. Because the rudder is unbalanced a long tiller is needed and this, together with the tapering of the hull, determines the position of the cabin. If the upper part of the stern is cut away, the traditional rudder could be removed and replaced by a much smaller balanced rudder mounted below a

For many years the paper makers John Dickinson & Company used pairs of FMC boats to handle the delivery of raw materials to its mills at Apsley, Nash, Home Park and Croxley in Hertfordshire and to take away the finished paper products. The boats were painted up in Dickinsons' colours as the steamer COUNTESS shown here at Bulls Bridge. (William Knibbs)

counter built out to the previous maximum overall length. Because a somewhat shorter tiller can be used the steerer can stand further back enabling the cabin to be built further back and so the hold can be made longer. It is only a matter of 18 inches or so, but it would represent an extra ton of cargo.

A further gain is that the underwater shape of the boat is improved, the screw being below the counter in free water instead of buried in the deadwood behind the original rudder. The modified hull could be expected to carry the extra ton of cargo without an increase in resistance whilst propeller efficiency would be increased and fuel consumption reduced. If, at the same time, a more modern power plant replaced the original one, the conversion might well achieve significant economies.

After an extended trial period EUROPE, the first steel boat, was scrapped as being worn out after only eight years in service, the

other four horse boats were sold for between £35 and £30 each after similar periods of time in the fleet and the steamer DUCHESS was sold to carriers at Abingdon in June 1893 for £575. After this experience no more steel boats were built and the Fazeley Street yard was closed down and its site was taken for the new canal basin and storage facilities.

With this closure, work on the steamers switched to Saltley where a re-building programme was instituted. In December 1893 PHOENIX, a wooden boat originally built in May 1884 at Tipton, was rebuilt and given a new wooden hull; the hull and reassembling the machinery costing £500. SPEEDWELL and PIRATE followed her in 1894 with new wooden hulls whilst EARL was built in 1895. In March 1895 the steel steamer DUKE was reconstructed for £500 with a wooden hull being provided.

In June 1896 PRINCESS was rebuilt with an iron composite hull

at a cost of £500. Walter Pollock, who was a partner in James Pollock & Sons, consulting engineers and naval architects, carried out the design work. He may also have been involved in the design of the steel steamers. Whatever, PRINCESS proved satisfactory in service resulting in the remaining two steel steamers, COUNTESS and EMPRESS, being rebuilt in June 1897 and May 1898 respectively.

The success of the iron composite hulls was such that FMC began to enlarge its steamer fleet by building new craft. The first, MARQUIS, was launched from Saltley in March 1898 at a cost of £600 and others followed on at intervals with the last, VICTORY, being completed in November 1911 at £600. Their arrival brought the steamer fleet up to 28 craft.

The early steamers had been fitted with engines and boilers from a variety of manufacturers but Fellows Morton and later FMC had introduced a major improvement in the engine used. The firm's engineer was William Howard Haines who had been born in 1857 to Job and Mary Haines; his sister Mary being married to Joshua Fellows. William patented an improved vertical tandem compound engine and this was manufactured at the Fazeley Street workshops and became the standard fitting for the steamer fleet. The boat's name was cast on the valve chest of the upper, or high pressure, cylinder and the company's name on the lower, or low pressure, cylinder together with the date. Exceptions were BARON and BARONESS both of which were fitted with engines built by Nettlefolds of Birmingham in 1898.

William was also a director of W. H. & A. H. Haines Limited, which was based in Lower Fazeley Street next to FMC and employed 200 men on the production of steam engines, steam compressors, steam refrigerators and other machinery. Its success owed much to William but he died prematurely in 1897

The office staff at Albion Wharf, Wolverhampton in 1926 showing, from left to right, a junior clerk, Mr E. R. Tart (assistant cashier), Mr William Bradshaw (superintendent of the Northern fleet that was based here), Miss Edith Wordsley (typist) and Harold Brooks Worboys (Chief Cashier & Office Manager). (Mrs N. Worboys)

The Clino staff car at Albion Wharf in 1927. This was shared by the two fleet superintendents – Harold Worboys and Mac Anderson. (Mrs N. Worboys)

aged forty.

The new engine entailed the use of higher steam pressures and, hence, an improved boiler was needed. Many of the steamers being built, or rebuilt, in the 1890s were fitted with a newly patented boiler produced by Cochranes of Birkenhead. Subsequently several boilers were used from Fletcher's Phoenix Foundry in Derby or from the Danks Foundry at Oldbury. In 1905

THE KING and the next three steamers were fitted with boilers produced by John Thompson & Co. Ltd. of Wolverhampton but PRESIDENT and the last four steamers all had boilers from Ruston Proctor & Co. Ltd. of Lincoln. The last four also had a new lightweight engine designed by Henry Rodolph De Salis, a director of the company, and manufactured by A. H. Beasley & Sons at Rockingham Ironworks in Uxbridge which enabled them to carry

LAPWING's cargo being unloaded at the Old Wharf, Bridge Street, Birmingham onto two Foden steam wagons, one with solid and the other with pneumatic tyres, and three 2-ton horse wagons in the early 1930s. (The Waterways Archive, Gloucester)

more weight.

Being compounds both types of engine normally ran on a condensing cycle, but provision was made for them to run non-condensing with the exhaust being discharged up the funnel. Normally boiler water was drawn from the canal or river through filters and a mud separator. These needed frequent cleaning when passing through shallow and weeded waterways. The run to Market Harborough was particularly difficult as in the summer a fine weed grew on the section between Foxton and the town and especially around Gallows Hill, and this blocked the inlet to the condenser. Usually weed could be raked out from the perforated copper grill that covered the inlet, which was about 18 inches above the bottom of the boat; this being part of the driver's job. The weed on the Harborough arm was too fine for this and the condenser had to be disconnected and run under high pressure until Foxton or Market Harborough was reached. Sometimes steamers carried a large 40-gallon drum which could

be assembled at the back end of the boat - it was for cooling purposes in weed infested waters, such as the Market Harborough arm, or in saline water such as in the north-west around Middlewich.

The boilers originally worked at a pressure of 100 pounds per square inch but several were subsequently altered to 110 psi whilst the Ruston Proctor boilers worked at 120 psi and sometimes this was increased to 130 psi or even to 140 psi in the case of VANGUARD.

The steamer boatmen always knew the steamers as "Engines". As the machinery weighed up to ten tons and took up a lot of space they could only carry about 12 tons of cargo. They burned coke, which was stored in the engine room in bunkers that extended down both sides of the lagged boiler and was as far forward as possible as no more weight was wanted aft to add to that of the boiler and engine. The coke could also be stored in front of the mast in 1cwt bags.

Ingots being loaded onto one of the company's Foden steam lorries at Crescent Wharf for onward delivery to a customer. (Birmingham Central Library)

Between 1¾ tons and 2 tons of coke were used on a round trip, the bunkers holding about a ton of fuel. Bunkering stations were maintained at Bulls Bridge, Braunston, Birmingham and Nottingham but that at Nottingham always caused problems as the coke came in large lumps, which wasted space, making it difficult to take on enough fuel.

All the steamers were fitted with a large propeller nearly 3-feet in diameter of coarse pitch to take advantage of the inherently good low speed torque of the steam engine. Some had specially shaped blades, which were developed with weed slipping properties. The maximum revolutions for the canals were 200 per minute, the propeller often drawing the whole stern end of the boat at this speed. The boats always ran with the bottom of the counter about 4 inches under the water to prevent the propeller sucking air down from the surface, which reduced efficiency. When working on deeper rivers, such as the Soar and Trent, a maximum of 300 rpm was possible. The Haines engine gave 11-shaft horsepower at 160 rpm.

For the most part the steamers operated on the express, or fly, services between London, Braunston, Birmingham, Leicester and Nottingham. At one time the Birmingham service was extended around the Black Country but it was soon withdrawn, as it did not prove a practical proposition. There was also a steamer run to Coventry but it was not as regular as the main routes, traffic mainly being from London with only occasional back loads – once just a 3-cwt garden roller.

The main steamer services operated to a strict timetable and it was against FMC's rules for them to stop. Boatmen knew to within a ¼-mile where they would meet their colleagues going the other way.

Normally a steamer with its accompanying butty had a crew of seven - four on the steamer and three on the butty. The

A boat being unloaded of her cargo of imported goods at Crescent Wharf. The crates would have been off loaded from ships in Liverpool Docks, lightered across the Mersey to Ellesmere Port, and there transferred to narrow boats. One of the crates originated from Uruguay. (Birmingham Central Library)

steamer crew comprised the captain, captain's mate, chief driver and assistant driver. The captain, who was sometimes called the chief captain, was responsible for the boats and cargo, employed and paid the other crew members. He always worked with the assistant driver and his mate with the chief driver.

Two men were always on duty on the steamer with changeovers being made at fixed points. On the City Road Basin to Fazeley Street run these were at Greenford, Uxbridge, Ironbridge lock Watford (No 77), Fishery lock Boxmoor (No 63), Cowroast lock (No 46), Neal's lock Slapton (No 30), Talbots lock Stoke Hammond (No 23), Bradwell Wharf, Stoke Bruerne top lock (No 14), Long Buckby top lock (No 7), Two Boats Inn Long Itchington, Hatton top lock and Knowle top lock. Going south some of the changeover points were slightly different.

On the shorter Brentford to Braunston run the steamer crew was usually three-handed dispensing with the assistant driver. At one time four pairs and two single steamers were on this run, each averaging three rounds trips a fortnight. At Braunston a transhipment depot and stables had been established and the steamers discharged their cargoes on arrival, reloaded, exchanged loaded butties and returned to Brentford. Four horse boats ran a shuttle service between Braunston and Birmingham and were known as the "Braunston Feeders".

The drivers lived and slept in the engine room, the steerer communicating by means of a bell. FMC supplied string hammocks, which were slung across the boats in front of the boiler. Even when working alone the driver could get some sleep - it was said a full head of steam at Itchington lock would take the boat the 8½ miles to Braunston. Most of the cooking was done in the engine room using the heat from the boiler. Often a stew would be set to cook when they left London and it would last until they reached Braunston.

Usually the crews wore white overalls and white cord trousers. These had to be changed at least once a week for clean ones - a charge of 6d (2½p) being made for laundering. The crews used to chew twist, tobacco made into a thick cord, which they then

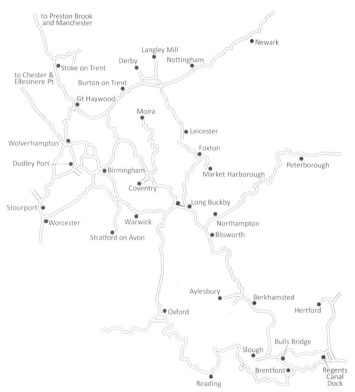

41

A busy scene at the Fazeley Street depot in the mid 1930s showing how the cluster of boats sometimes virtually blocked the canal. (Author's Collection)

stuffed into their trouser pockets, causing unsightly yellow stains. The tailors Penningtons of Brentford supplied cords all over the waterways. The order with measurements would be passed from boatman to boatman until it got to Brentford. The finished trousers found their way back to the purchaser in the same way, as did the payment to Penningtons.

In the engine room, where it was naturally very hot, the drivers wore thin blue overalls and jackets, which they called "blue slop". Normally the boats were kept very clean, some drivers being so proud they used to hang a curtain between the boiler and engine during firing to prevent coke dust falling on the engine.

On the steamer run the butty crew were responsible for

dealing with the various toll offices passed en route, for dealing with swing bridges of which there were once considerable numbers between London and Birmingham, and for all lock-wheeling.

Women were not usually allowed on the steamers, except during holidays and then only with special permission. The company had to make an exception to this rule during the last two years of the First World War when many of the men had been called up. Several steamers were then worked two-handed with the husband as captain and his wife as driver. They still worked non-stop and some wives drove much faster than their men folk. Indeed one was reported to have taken her boat straight through

Standing on VANGUARD's counter outside the Fazeley Street Depot, the fleet superintendent Mac Anderson (in the bowler hat) is accompanied by director John Ironmonger (in the trilby hat). The other boats were motors HAWK and ROVER and butty QUEBEC. (The Waterways Archive, Gloucester)

the shallow lock at Fenny Stratford without stopping whilst her husband was asleep in the engine room. Many of the men were married and a large number had houses in Braunston.

On the Birmingham run the steamers often dropped off their butties at Braunston and then carried on alone because of the narrow locks on the two Warwick canals. The butties followed close behind in charge of a horse, the pair being reunited above Hatton top lock to complete the journey through to Fazeley Street wharf. Sometimes, however, the crew would manhandle the butty through the narrow locks. The horse changeover points were fixed at Hatton and Braunston as otherwise the butties would have had to be manhandled through Shrewley tunnel and the company already had stables at Braunston.

The boats on the Birmingham run often carried cargoes of soap and the other boatmen called their crews "greasy-wheelers" or "greasy-ockers". The name "ocker" derived from Ocker Hill where FMC once had an office. The crews of the Leicester and Nottingham boats were called "woolly-backed ones" - a name

43

Two of the collection of horse drawn delivery vehicles that FMC maintained at the Crescent Wharf in Birmingham to handle the delivery of cargoes from, and to, the narrow boat fleet. (Birmingham Central Library)

believed to be associated with the Leicester wool trade.

The normal time for the City Road Basin to Fazeley Street trip was about 54 hours and the boats used to do 52 round trips a year, even allowing for the time tied up for holidays. This was a stiff schedule for which the crews were specially picked. Two steamers left Birmingham each night and two left London.

On the run there were a series of transhipping places where goods could be dropped off and picked up. At these places there were often little stone buildings with one set of doors leading out onto the canal and another out onto the road. It had been known for a steamer to change its entire load in the course of a single trip. If there were several places to call at it really put the crews on their mettle to maintain the tight schedule.

These transhipping places were at Greenford, Bulls Bridge,

FMC sold DUCHESS in 1893 to traders based at Abingdon but subsequently she was acquired by Thornycrofts of Reading who fitted her up with an experimental gas engine. She is shown here at Brentford prior to starting on a trial run to Birmingham. (Author's collection)

Packet Boat Bridge (Cowley Peachey), Uxbridge, Rickmansworth, Cassio Bridge (Watford), Hunton Bridge top, Boxmoor, Berkhamsted, Cowroast, Marsworth Arm End, Church Lock, Leighton Buzzard, Water End (Fenny Stratford), Simpson Wharf, Pear Tree (Woughton), Red Sheds (Woolstone), Great Linford, Bradwell, Wolverton, Yardley Gobion, bottom of Stoke, Gayton Arm End, Banbury Lane, High Heyford, top of Buckby, Welton, Braunston (main depot), Shuckburgh, Blue Lias (Stockton), bottom of Radford, Emscote, Rowington, Black Boy (Heronfield), top of Knowle, Catherine de Barnes and Acocks Green. On the Leicester run there were transhipping places at Crick, Yelvertoft, North Kilworth and Blaby.

Another regular steamer run was from either Brentford or City Road Basin to Leicester, Nottingham and Derby; it was known as the Nottingham Fly. Sugar from London was a regular cargo, with perfume from the Boots factory in Nottingham often making up a return load for the steamer, which might then pick up its butty loaded with iron pipes from Stantons near Ilkeston, at Trent lock

at the mouth of the Erewash Canal. A wide variety of tinned and packaged goods was also handled. Here again with the narrow locks on the old Grand Union Canal between Norton and Foxton, the steamers dropped off their butties at Buckby top lock, where FMC had some stables just below the lock, and carried on alone, often to their destinations.

The steamers used to take only 4½ hours to traverse the Twenty Mile Pound between Watford and Foxton. With the greater depth on the river sections the boats could move even faster and they would still work up river even if it was in a fair state of flood. At these times the locks on the Beeston Cut often had only about a 12 to 18 inches rise and the boats would be able to bang the gates open without stopping. When the Soar was in flood the steamers had to run with the funnel down because of several low bridges.

With their great power the steamers made ideal ice-breaking craft; they were supposed to be able to break ice up to 5 inches thick although this was frowned on by the company owing to

The gas boat VULCAN pictured at the end of 1908 near Saltley Dock (Birmingham Central Library)

possible damage to the hull and to the large propeller. The boats were well maintained by FMC with docking taking place about every three years.

In March 1911 FMC launched the experimental wide steamer SWAN from its Uxbridge boatyard. She was 72-feet long and 10½-feet wide and was designed to carry 34 tons. Her engine and boiler were made by T. A. Savery & Co. Ltd. of Newcomen Works, Bracebridge Street, Birmingham. The engine was an open compound surface-condensing quick-running type and developed between 45 and 50 horsepower at 600 rpm on a pressure of 250 psi. The engine was placed forward of the boiler so as to prevent heat reaching the cargo, to keep weight over the stern and to keep the cabin warm. Built of wood, SWAN was fitted with a special weed-slipping propeller whose design resulted from FMC's considerable practical experience in this field.

The boiler was a standard straight water tube type with the tubes expanded into steel drums and it was oil fired using refuse oil, tar or gas oil. A copper tube condenser was located under the counter and fuel tanks, containing up to 400 gallons of oil were located either side of the boiler. There were pressure oil tanks on either side of the engine room, which held 40 gallons and were pressurised at 40 psi. Pumps for feed water and condenser evacuation were driven off the main crankshaft whilst the air compressor for fuel pressure was driven off the tail rod of the low-pressure cylinder. The total weight of the machinery including engine, boiler, stern gear and condensers but excluding oil tanks and fuel was some 31cwt.

Commissioned in August 1911, by January 1912 SWAN had logged over 4,500 miles or 2,250 hours steaming - equivalent to about twenty-four return journeys from Brentford to Braunston. Despite this the boat was not deemed a success, possibly because of the more restricted channel northwards from Berkhamsted, which saw few wider beam craft. As a result the machinery was eventually taken out and the hull was sold to J. W. Winship who

A busy scene at Saltley Dock in 1903 with what would become EGYPT being built in the foreground, an unidentified boat undergoing repairs behind on the left, the nearly completed NATAL on the right and several other boats behind. (Mrs Smallwood, daughter of Mark Gould, one time foreman of the dock)

LYNX, one of the initial batch of iron composite motor boats, poses probably soon after her launch from FMC's Saltley boatyard in 1913. (The Waterways Archive, Gloucester)

intended to install a National diesel engine.

During the First World War the steamers carried munitions to various destinations one of which was the important Weedon Ordnance Depot in Northamptonshire. There was a strict rule that all fires had to be put out before boats passed under the portcullis into the fortified part of the depot to reach the magazines at the far end of the branch canal. In practice it seems everything was shut down so that there was no sign of the fire, with glib lies being told to the military. As the steamers burned coke, there was no smoke.

This ruse reduced turn round times considerably and gave the crews more free time when they returned to the City Road Basin. Here the pubs were open from 5am to 12.30pm, which allowed them plenty of time for drinking. Rum was a favourite tipple, being consumed in large quantities and brought in quart bottles for consumption on the trip. After the war the steamers were used to carry scrap munitions, often from Regent's Canal Dock, back to the various military depots. But by the end of the war the days of the steamers were numbered.

CHAPTER FOUR
THE COMPANY GROWS

Following the formation of FMC some wooden boats continued to be built and repaired at Tipton, one of the last being SCOTLAND launched in January 1890 at a cost of £160. Thereafter most new building work switched to Saltley, DAISY being launched from there in January 1891 costing £150 as the first in a series of boats with girl's names. In 1894 a number of wooden boats named mainly after towns served by the canals started to appear, the first being WEDNESBURY in April costing £160.

In 1894 the company ventured into metal construction again when AUSTRALIA was launched from Saltley in July at a cost of £175. She was of iron composite construction with an elm bottom, pitch pine kelson, iron sides and an oak gunwale and followed the previous practice of naming metal boats after continents. AUSTRALIA proved to be much more successful than the steel boats and was used initially for station boating – transhipment work to and from canal-connected railway basins on the Birmingham Canal Navigations – before being fitted up as a regular butty in May 1903.

This development led FMC to undertake a major expansion to the modest facilities at Saltley with the aim of building up the production of metal boats, concentrating repair work there and enabling the Tipton yard to be closed. On 17 August 1895 an agreement was signed by Thomas Clayton for FMC and William Salt for the Birmingham and Warwick Junction Canal for a new dry dock to be constructed at Park Wharf, Duddeston Road, Saltley with the land being leased at the modest rental of £25 per annum. Construction followed and the large covered dock, capable of holding a number of boats simultaneously, was opened in 1896.

Wooden town class boats continued to be built at Saltley until June 1897 when DUDLEY was launched at £160, but then most production switched to composite construction with LEIGHTON being launched in January 1898 at a cost of £200 as the first iron boat since AUSTRALIA, except for some tar boats possibly built for Thomas Clayton. Throughout 1898 an iron composite boat appeared every month but production slowed down in the following years and even included a few wooden boats such as KINGSWOOD in February 1901 at £160. The last wooden boat to be built at Saltley was FLINT launched in January 1906 with an elm bottom, a pitch pine kelson, larch sides, oak linings and a fore-end

LINDA undergoing repairs at the Saltley Dock in 1923. LINDA was the company's first motor boat and was commissioned from the same dock on 17 April 1912 with a 15bhp Bolinder direct reversing crude oil Model E engine which, with the propeller, cost £189. In February 1930 an improved Model BM engine was fitted here at Saltley. (Cheshire Record Office)

The plate off the steamer HECLA that was built at Uxbridge in 1923 during a period when there was a shortage of Bolinder diesel engines, prompting a limited return to steam power. (Author's Collection)

of spruce all for the remarkably low price of £120.

In January 1903 Saltley launched PRETORIA, the first of a class of iron composite boats all named after places overseas. The class eventually totalled 30 craft, the last being VIENNA in February 1911.

In October 1896 FMC purchased Edwin Morgan's boat building yard, known as Grand Junction Dock, and premises for a coal wharf at Uxbridge, just south of the road carrying the Slough Road over the canal. The Grand Junction agreed to take over the freehold for £1,325 and to spend a further £2,500 on modernising the existing buildings and erecting new ones. FMC was then granted a 21-year lease and went on to develop the yard's boat building and repair operations and to establish a wholesale coal department, which ultimately was separated to become a wholly-owned subsidiary company. Under its new owners the first boat to be built was the appropriately named UXBRIDGE in June 1897 at a cost of £150 followed by a series of wooden town class boats starting with AYLESBURY and FENNY in January 1898.

Towards the end of 1899 the Uxbridge yard was hired out to Alfred James Ash, who had a boatyard at Great Bridge, and he went on to build 20 wooden boats for the company all named after trees. The first, ASH, was launched in January 1900 at a cost of £170 – she had an elm bottom, pitch pine kelson, with sides, linings and gunwales of oak. The batch was completed with WALNUT a year later in January 1901, by which time Ash had taken over as chairman of FMC.

Uxbridge then resumed production of town class butties which continued until JARROW was launched in April 1912 at a cost of £150. In March 1910 ALICE was launched being followed two months later by KATE both being destined for an important traffic operated for John Dickinson & Co. Ltd. Another special building was the launch of the wide boat BRAUNSTON in November 1910 costing £145. She was 70ft 2in long, 10ft 5in wide at the top and 8ft wide at the bottom and was followed by HAREFIELD, ISLINGTON and ISLEWORTH of similar dimensions. All four saw service at the southern end of the Grand Junction Canal,

The steamer HECLA featured prominently in the 1923 boatman's strike at Braunston. Here a group of the strikers on her stern pose for the camera. (William Knibbs)

such as to Toovey's mill at Kings Langley, where their greater carrying capacity was a major advantage over narrow boats.

There was an important development in 1912 when to relieve the pressure of work on the Saltley yard the company ordered two dozen iron composite butty boats from Braithwaite & Kirk of West Bromwich at £190 each. The first to emerge in May was GRANGE and the rest followed in a near alphabetical sequence ending with YARMOUTH in May 1914.

They were not the first boats from an outside builder as in February 1899 CHELFORD had arrived from Rathbone Brothers of Stretford costing £170 and she was followed by two others. Also in 1899 POLLY and WOBBY were built by W. E. Costin Ltd. at Berkhamsted Dock although a Mrs. Thomas seems to have had an interest in them, which she passed over to FMC in 1907. Costins also produced MONTGOMERY and MERIONETH in 1906 for £140 each whilst Worsey Ltd. which had several yards in the West Midlands, built USK in November 1911 for £150.

During all this time FMC had continued to grow, not only through the building of new craft, but also by taking over other carrying businesses. One of the most important was the old-established and profitable coal and carrying business operated by Samuel Phipkin who was based at the Forresters Arms, Starveall, West Drayton from where he operated a fleet of narrow boats and some wide beam craft. FMC took over his business in two tranches – the first was in April 1890 when some 15 narrow boats were acquired whilst another 15 narrow boats and three wide beam craft followed in June 1897. Phipkin gave up as he was elderly and wanted to be relieved of running the business but he agreed to remain as a consultant to FMC. He took part of the purchase price in shares holding 50 ordinary and 50 preference shares but died not long after giving up.

In October 1893 four boats operated by Cudlipp & Co. Ltd. of Little Eaton near Derby were acquired, followed in the summer of 1894 by the business of Alfred Landon based in the City Road Basin

OLDBURY, EGYPT, RAMBLER and AIRE were moored opposite the entrance to the boat yard arm at Braunston during the 1923 strike. (Ike Argent collection)

and involving four boats. Landon had been the agent for the London & Midlands Counties Carrying Company but had continued trading on his own account after that concern was acquired by Fellows Morton. He was connected with John and Henry Landon who were carriers trading mainly to and from Aylesbury.

Two years later the small business of George Hurst & Sons of Northampton and Leighton Buzzard was taken over. Hurst had been in business for 20 years having taken on some of the Grand Junction's traffic. His boats now joined the fleet, FMC also gaining a leased wharf and premises in Northampton, situated on the northern arm of the river Nene, and a small base at Leighton Buzzard. FMC acquired the freehold of the Northampton premises in 1907.

A more substantial acquisition came in July 1898 when 17 narrow boats were purchased from the London & Birmingham Canal Carrying Co. Ltd. It had been formed in about August 1890 as successors to Joseph Wiles & Son of St. Albans in Hertfordshire and had operated two steamers – ANTELOPE and BUFFALO – in addition to its unpowered craft. The steamers did not pass to FMC but were sold to William Mead & Company of Paddington who used them extensively on towing duties at the southern end of the Grand Junction. Another small purchase was from William Phipkin and William Palmer of Yiewsley in February 1899 with

JAPAN & KILSBY at Braunston during the 1923 boatmen's strike. (Ike Argent)

some eight boats being taken over.

A new era started in 1912 when FMC launched LINDA, its first motor-driven boat, from Saltley on 17 April. LINDA had an identical hull to the iron composite steamers but was fitted with a 15hp single cylinder direct-reversing semi-diesel engine manufactured by the Swedish company of J. & C. G. Bolinder of Stockholm and imported by their United Kingdom agents James Pollock Sons & Co. Ltd., which later became established at Faversham in Kent. Again Walter Pollock was actively involved in the design of the craft and the fitting of their engines. LINDA's hull and cabin works cost £600 and the engine – an "E" type Bolinder – a further £189.

FMC was not the first to introduce motor boats on the canals. In August 1907 Edward Tailby of Birmingham had launched PROGRESS which was powered by a paraffin engine and in July 1911 Cadbury Brothers of Bournville, Birmingham had the

purpose-built steel-hulled BOURNVILLE 1 fitted with a 15hp Bolinder. There were also several pioneers at the southern end of the Grand Junction Canal, such as Emanuel Smith of Brentford, but it was through FMC that motor boats came into widespread use, the company remaining faithful to Bolinders throughout its existence.

LINDA was followed by LEOPARD and a further eight craft ending with LUPIN in March 1914 whilst the Uxbridge yard produced the wooden LINDOLA in August 1912, which cost £450 and was fitted with a 10hp Bolinder. LINDOLA was first tried on the Wolverhampton to Preston Brook run but was transferred to working to and from Northampton. Whilst the war tended to slow developments down a few more motors continued to be built.

On 15 October 1890 FMC took on what was to become a very important and prestigious contract – the transport of raw materials

With a strong contingent of police lined up to keep order Mac Anderson, in plus fours, the superintendent of the Southern fleet, discusses the situation of the man on the ground, who had been thrown into the canal, with Mr Brooks, the official from the Transport & General Workers Union. This took place following an attempt by the company to offload the cargo from some of the boats involved in the strike. (The Waterways Archive, Gloucester)

Steamers HECLA and SPEEDWELL and other FMC boats tied up in the boatyard arm at Braunston during the 1923 boatmen's strike. (William Knibbs)

from London to John Dickinson & Co. Ltd's mills at Croxley, Home Park, Nash and Apsley in the river Gade valley in Hertfordshire and the distribution of the company's finished paper products from the mills. As part of the new arrangement FMC purchased at least two boats from Dickinsons as these were now redundant. Initially only horse-drawn narrow boats were involved and they worked to a regular timetable with deliveries and collections being made at set times. The schedule down to Dickinsons depot at Paddington and back was very tight involving high speeds and the boats quickly became known as "The Paper Boats" or "The Paper Mill Dashers".

In 1892 consideration was being given to introducing a wide boat on the service but as this would not move as quickly as the narrow boats Dickinsons were asked to agree to allow an additional two hours from Croxley down to London. A trial with

ORWELL was then carried out but even this extra allowance was insufficient; instead FMC supplied a fourth narrow boat to provide the extra capacity needed. Soon after FMC introduced a steamer onto the service to maintain the tight schedule involved and this operated on alternate days with its butty.

From 1 January 1897 horse haulage was given up with a second steamer and butty being put on to provide a daily service between Apsley and Paddington with the butties being picked up and dropped off at Croxley. A pair left Apsley at 4pm each weekday and called at Nash, Home Park and Croxley before reaching Paddington at midnight. The boats always stopped at Uxbridge over the weekends so that any maintenance could be carried out.

These boats were hired out to Dickinsons and painted up in

A group of boatmen gathered round Mr. Brooks, their union official, at Braunston during the 1923 boatmen's strike. (Ike Argent)

Dickinsons colours, the first steamers being COUNTESS and PRINCESS whilst the butties ALICE and KATE were built in 1910 at Uxbridge especially for this traffic. An oval brass plate was carried in the engine room or on the butty's hatch covers recording FMC's ownership. In the year ended 31 March 1901 10,468 tons were handled. An inter-mill service was also provided with FMC building the open wide boats APSLEY and CROXLEY for this in 1896.

A new agreement was signed on 1 January 1905 whereby FMC was allowed to charge 3/3d (16p) per ton up to 8,000 tons per annum and all over at 2/9d (14p) per ton. If the traffic exceeded 11,000 tons a 2½% discount was to be allowed. In May 1927 the steamers were replaced by motors – in July 1930 JACKAL & HELEN and JAGUAR & HETTIE were on the run but later the butties were replaced by YARDLEY and YIEWSLEY as the wooden boats were getting knocked about so much.

The traffic to the mills comprised paper making materials such as rags, waste and shavings that was collected from Paddington whilst Dickinsons well-known brands of paper and board travelled southwards from the mills. The traffic figures between 1904 and 1930 have survived – northbound an average of 5,300 tons were carried each year, the highest year being 1910 with 6,695 tons and the highest month being July 1908 with 777 tons. Southbound the average was 7,240 tons with the highest year being 1916 with 9,350 tons and the highest month being April with 979 tons.

An area where Joshua Fellows was particularly keen to develop traffic was on the route to Leicester and beyond. As early as August 1891 the Grand Junction Canal Company had inspected the Old Union and the Grand Union Canals that made up the route from Norton to Leicester with a view to a possible

To show solidarity with their men folk, a group of wives and their children at Braunston pose for the camera during the 1923 boatmen's strike. (Ike Argent)

purchase and steps to boost traffic. It offered £5,000 for the two canals in January 1892 but this was rejected.

In May 1893 Joshua Fellows asked that the qualifying level for FMC's rebate on Leicester Line traffic should be reduced from £1,000 to £800 due to the poor condition of the Grand Union Canal, which was restricting the amount of cargo that boats could carry. He predicted that if nothing was done traffic would drop significantly and suggested the Grand Junction should purchase the two canals and improve the navigation to Leicester. The reduction was agreed and the Grand Junction indicated it was willing to reconsider the purchases if FMC would guarantee an increased level of traffic once improvements had been completed.

There were further discussions with Fellows in June as he had been offered the two Union canals for £20,000 and he was authorised to act as the Grand Junction's agent to purchase them with all their freehold and leasehold properties, plant and water rights for no more than this figure. In July he had agreed to acquire the Grand Union Canal for £10,500, the Old Union for £6,500 with a further £250 being paid to the companies' clerk as compensation for loss of office. The Act of Parliament authorising the purchase was assented on 20 July 1894 and the transfer took place of 29 September. The Grand Junction went on to obtain options to purchase the Leicester and Loughborough Navigations and the Erewash Canal to give it control of the canal route north of Leicester.

An extensive dredging work, estimated to cost £27,250, now got under way with a new dredger and hopper boats being purchased and by the end of 1895 nearly £7,000 had been spent. From 1 July 1895 FMC was granted a 10% rebate on traffic over £5,000 per annum and 15% over £8,000 for a seven-year term.

57

A crowd of boat people gathered round AUSTRALIA at the entrance to the boat yard arm at Braunston during the 1923 boatmen's strike. (Ike Argent)

In February 1896 FMC suggested the flights of narrow locks at Watford and Foxton should be widened to enable wide beam craft to work through as this would reduce costs and enable it to increase the traffic between London, Leicester and Nottingham. As evidence of its commitment the company had the wide boat TRENT built by Rudkins of Leicester in May 1897 and she was followed by AYLESTONE in September whilst the wide boat ELIZABETH was recorded for Joshua's brother, John Fellows of Barnt Green in Worcestershire, in October. FMC had intended to build at least five of these wide-beam craft but whilst the Grand Junction had now decided to replace the ten narrow locks at Foxton with an inclined plane lift capable of handling two narrow boats side-by-side, it had made no decision about widening the seven narrow locks at Watford.

In February 1900 a plan to widen the Watford locks at a cost of £17,000 was accepted but no work was started pending completion of the Foxton lift. This was opened on 10 July 1900 and FMC's steamer PHOENIX was reported to have been the first working boat to use it. In practice the lift was not as successful as hoped, the Watford locks were not widened and FMC's wide boats were confined to working between Gainsborough, Nottingham, Leicester and Market Harborough and were soon sold.

With the development work FMC was undertaking and the growth in its fleet extra capital soon became necessary. A further call of £2 per share had been made on the partly-paid ordinary shares at the end of 1890 or early 1891 and the final £2 call was made on 9 October 1891 making the 5,962 shares fully paid. An extra 544 ordinary shares were issued in 1898, some being to Samuel Phipkin, increasing the number to 6,506. Meanwhile the number of preference shares had peaked at 3,000 in 1898 but declined slightly soon after.

In September 1898 £20,000 of a new 4% debenture was issued to help finance a major extension to the company's premises at the City Road Basin. Elsewhere there had been a rolling programme of improvements. By 1895 the leases of both the company's warehouses in Nottingham had expired and to replace them it acquired a 99-year lease of a plot of land in Canal Street from Nottingham Corporation in June. On this a large warehouse with offices and stables was completed in the following year, enabling FMC's business to be concentrated on one site. This led

The motor boats CAMEL and CORMORANT under construction at the Northwich yard of W. J. Yarwood & Sons Ltd early in 1924. (Cheshire Record Office)

to a significant increase in its Nottingham traffic.

At Brentford the company agreed in May 1889 to take over the wharf and premises previously occupied by Whitehouse & Son on a 21-year lease at £100 per annum. The Grand Junction repaired the wharf wall, put the cranes in order, provided stabling and carried out other improvements with FMC paying interest on the capital sum spent. In 1897 the storage facilities at Brentford were extended with the Grand Junction investing some £2,500 on FMC's property in exchange for increased rent. This was part of a much larger scheme to develop Brentford as an inland port and included duplicating the gauging lock. The Grand Junction also offered to provide similar storage accommodation at Paddington but the

An unidentified steamer with its butty PINE head north at Weedon. (Railway & Canal Historical Society – from a postcard postmarked 22 July 1905)

Regent's Canal Company agreed to grant FMC a new fifty-year lease for the City Road Basin premises at the previous rental of £500 provided FMC spent £5,000 on new buildings, and the new lease was sealed on 11 October 1898.

By now the company had inherited or established a chain of depots and agencies to handle its growing trade. For instance the former Grand Junction Canal depot at Dudley Port was taken on lease in August 1890 at £160 per annum whilst in about 1896 an agency was established at Pleck Wharf, Walsall and another at Emscote, Warwick where the agent was Mr. A. Lighton.

Another move was prompted by the opening of the Manchester Ship Canal in 1894, FMC being appointed to act as the new concern's agent in the Midlands, which was expected to lead to a large increase in trade. To maximise on this new opportunity an office was opened in Manchester and Frederick Morton moved from Wolverhampton to take charge of operations in the north-west where he was successful in securing the anticipated increase in trade.

By the end of the century the company had branches at Birmingham, Brentford, City Road Basin, Dudley Port, Leicester, Leighton Buzzard, Manchester, Northampton, Nottingham, Saltley, Uxbridge, Wolverhampton with agencies at Coventry, Derby, Hull, Liverpool, Walsall, Warwick and on the Manchester Ship Canal.

A serious problem arose in 1902 when the Grand Junction Canal experienced a major water shortage, which severely limited the number of boats it could pass over its Tring summit in Hertfordshire. Long delays, often running into many days, were experienced by all carriers and to try and alleviate the situation FMC was forced to divert many of its boats to the Thames and the Oxford Canal. This was a much longer and more expensive route giving increased journey times and wear and tear on the craft and horses. From the end of September 1902 through to the beginning of January 1903 the Grand Junction through route was severely restricted.

Through the Fellows family interests FMC had inherited a significant share holding in the Severn & Canal Carrying Co. Ltd. Following approval given by the shareholders at the annual general meeting on 25 July 1904 FMC's directors took steps to acquire a large block of shares in the Severn concern giving it outright control. At the time Severn & Canal operated a very profitable towing service on the river, which subsidised its less profitable carrying operations.

The Sharpness New Docks & Gloucester & Birmingham Navigation Company objected to this state of affairs as it believed

The horse boat ORANGE loaded with casks of vinegar lies sunk in the cutting a few hundred yards north of Blisworth tunnel after hitting an obstacle near Banbury Lane, some three miles north from here. BUCKINGHAM is alongside the ironstone loading wharf. The timber bridge carried a railway from the ironstone quarry. (The Waterways Archive, Gloucester)

it was unfair competition on other traders and on whom the dock company depended. Early in 1906 the dock company put two tugs on the Severn to compete and this caused FMC to sell its Severn & Canal shares, but it continued to appoint a director. This brought about an unwritten agreement whereby FMC boats rarely traded down onto the Severn and Severn & Canal boats rarely ventured beyond Birmingham and Wolverhampton.

During all this time FMC traded profitably paying its ordinary shareholders an average dividend of 6% between 1890 and 1914

whilst maintaining the preference dividend at 6%. The highest profit was £19,458 in the year ended 30 September 1914 and the lowest was a mere £107 in 1892 when no dividends could be paid, although the preference holders got a double payment in 1893 to catch up. This poor result was due to severe competition causing a reduced volume of traffic coupled with lower freight rates, increased wages for the boatmen and higher lighterage costs. The previous year had also produced a disappointing result but this was due to most of the canals being closed for eight weeks by

A cluster of FMC boats – EGYPT, EXHALL, PRETORIA GAMBIA and LILAC – are moored above the Gauging Locks No 100 at Brentford. (David McDougall – from a postcard postmarked 1911)

frost throughout virtually all of December 1890 and January 1891.

A significant appointment was made on 30 July 1897 when Henry Rodolph de Salis joined the board as a director and he also became engineer to the company. He is best known for a series of extensive voyages over most of the country's inland waterways following which he produced his "Handbook of Inland Navigation - Bradshaw's Canals and Navigable Rivers of England and Wales".

De Salis was born on 30 June 1866, was educated at Eton and became an Associate Member of the Institution of Civil Engineers. His journeyings are thought to have started in 1887 in a steam-powered Thames-type launch called DRAGONFLY, which was 33-feet long, 6¾-feet wide and drew 2¾-feet. De Salis was usually accompanied by a friend and two boatmen on his travels. On 22 October 1891 he is known to have steamed through Sapperton Tunnel on the Thames & Severn Canal, the journey taking fifty minutes. In the following year a trip starting from Kingston-on-Thames on 11 June lasted a month and covered 730 miles with 450 locks and 7 major tunnels.

In May 1895 the original boat was replaced by a specially constructed steam powered narrow boat named DRAGONFLY II which was 59-feet long, 6¾-feet wide and drew 2½-feet. Thomas Clayton had been involved with the design of the boat, which was built at Abingdon in Berkshire. In a trip starting on 17 June 1895 and lasting two months 1,013 miles were covered involving 674 locks. By the end of 1896 De Salis had covered over 10,131 miles of inland waterway passing through 5,125 locks, 84 tunnels and a boat lift. By September 1901, when it is believed his trips ceased, the total had risen to 14,340 miles.

One of the original directors, Henry Williams, resigned from FMC's board on 26 August 1892 due to a serious illness and he died in February 1897, his place eventually being taken by De Salis.

On 11 March 1899 Reuben Farley, FMC's chairman, died and

A cluster of FMC and other carriers' boats line the canal during a stoppage at Long Buckby. Whilst FMC had stables for the horses, on occasions like these the limited space was soon taken up and many horses had to be kept on the towpath. (The Waterways Archive, Gloucester)

Colonel Alfred Ash took his place. Farley was the largest shareholder in the company with 237 preference and 400 ordinary shares to his name. Colonel Ash held 22 preference and 300 ordinary shares but he only remained in the chair for just over a year resigning on 20 September 1900. His place on the board and in the chair was taken by Alfred James Ash of Barnt Green from 2 November 1900. Ash, who held 150 preference and 125 ordinary shares at the time, was involved in the metal industry in Birmingham being a director of Ash & Lacy Ltd. and other companies. In 1905 he moved to Packwood House, Warwickshire, which he had bought at auction as a home for his 16-year old son Graham.

The next change occurred on 23 April 1900 when Joshua Fellows, probably the best remembered of all FMC's directors, died at his home at Woodville, Barnt Green from heart disease after a long spell of ill health; he was 66 years old. With his wife Mary he had moved to Barnt Green probably in 1897. Apart from his major involvement with FMC he was chairman of Sandwell Park Colliery Co. Ltd., a director of the Severn & Canal Carrying Co. Ltd, of W. Roberts Ltd. of Tipton and of John Bagnall & Sons Ltd., which no doubt resulted from his early dealings with Thomas Bagnall.

He had also been a director of the short-lived City of Birmingham Bank, which was taken over by Midland Bank early in 1899. The new bank had only been formed in 1897 and FMC had transferred its account to its Cannon Street, Birmingham branch from Lloyds Bank's branch in Birmingham's High Street. At the time of his death Joshua held 400 ordinary shares in FMC; his executors were his widow Mary and Richard, one of his sons.

Joshua was a great champion for the inland waterways, for canal carrying in general and for FMC in particular. In the early

John Ironmonger and Henry de Salis on LAMPREY in September 1934. The boat was undergoing trials with a new type of propeller. (Mrs N. Worboys)

1890s he assisted the Warwick and Birmingham Canal Company in a campaign to secure concessions for an agreed through toll rate for traffic between London and South Staffordshire rather than having to negotiate with the individual canal companies involved. The Board of Trade was the overseeing body and the rates were then laid down in a series of Canal Rates, Tolls and Charges Order Confirmation Acts passed in 1893 and 1894. The new through toll rate came into effect for the London to Birmingham run on 1 January 1895 largely as a result of Joshua's efforts. He went on to obtain through tolls from the midlands to Gloucester, Liverpool, Manchester and the Humber.

Joshua's death was followed by the resignation of Thomas Clayton from the board on 28 September 1900 on account of ill health. He held 25 preference and 406 ordinary shares at the time

but he continued to be involved in canal carrying with his own business being incorporated to become Thomas Clayton (Oldbury) Limited in 1904.

One of these two vacancies on the board was filled by the appointment of Henry Thomas Nock of Harborne who remained on the board until 10 November 1911.

By now the only one of the 1889 directors remaining on the board was Frederick Morton. His original agreement with the company as managing director had expired but he remained on the board as an ordinary director. It was he who was called upon to give evidence on behalf of FMC to the Royal Commission on Canals and Inland Waterways that was set up in 1906. In June 1906 he told the commission that FMC owned 229 horses on the fly boat services that worked with double crews round the clock using

Henry Rodolph de Salis, the company's engineering director, standing in the fore hatch of LAMPREY whilst the boat was on a test run from Sampson Road, Birmingham, out to Knowle in September 1934. (Mrs N. Worboys)

relays of horses. The company's business in fast consignments and parcels was expanding so rapidly, however, that even this number was insufficient and the company constantly had to hire in horses from other carriers.

With Thomas Clayton's departure Alfred Ironmonger took over much of the management of FMC's affairs and although he was not appointed as a director he acted as company secretary. He had joined the business at an early stage and is believed to have married into the Fellows family; he was certainly one of the coffin bearers at Joshua's funeral along with four of Joshua's son and

Charles Jones, another senior executive with the company. Ironmonger was in charge of the fleet and was a strict disciplinarian but he was much respected by the boatmen and their families.

CHAPTER FIVE
WORLD WAR ONE AND THE 1920S

The outbreak of the First World War on 28 July 1914 soon had an adverse effect on the company. As the war developed there was increasing disruption to the normal patterns of trade together

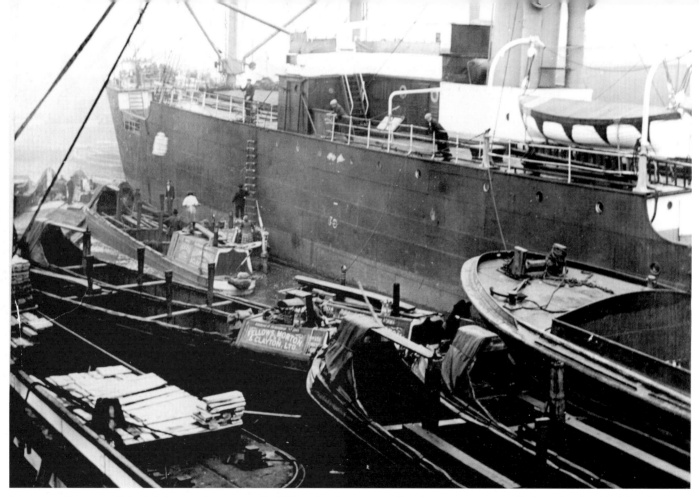

Four pairs of the company's boats in Regent's Canal Dock in the 1930s waiting to load cargo direct from sea-going ships. The boats include BARON & COLUMBIA and the motor PENGUIN. (The Waterways Archive, Gloucester)

with a steady drain of boatmen either enlisting, being conscripted into the army or leaving to work in munitions factories where higher wages were offered. To try and stem the exodus FMC was forced to pay higher wages or war bonuses, which led to greatly increased costs that it was not able to recoup as charging levels had been pegged. The war created a huge demand for transport and the level of traffic handled, particularly on busy canals like the Grand Junction, was maintained and even increased for some commodities but it was not profitable. At the end of December 1916 the company had showed a positive profit and loss balance of £11,170 and capital resources of over £135,000, but two years later the capital resources had dropped to below £108,000.

FMC's position was not unique being shared by most leading carriers and belatedly the government recognised the position and used its powers under the 1914 Defence of the Realm Regulations for the Board of Trade to set up a Canal Control Committee from 1 March 1917. This assumed control of most of the canals and many of the carriers with compensation being paid for loss of profits. The compensation was based on the last trading figures for each business prior to the war and for FMC this was to 30 September 1913 when the gross carrying revenue had been £161,081, expenses £146,328 and the profit £14,753 - some £68.18.9 (£68.94) for each of the 214 boats in service.

Figures for fifteen months to 31 December 1917 showed gross carrying revenue greatly reduced to £102,923, expenses of £99,090 and a net profit of £3,833, which entitled FMC to £5,213 compensation. For the 12 months to 31 December 1918 revenue was £163,290, expenses greatly increased to £164,106 giving a £816 loss and £14,511 compensation. In addition the company's non-carrying activities were compensated with £669 being paid for 1917 and £1,719 for 1918. Government control eventually came to an end on 31 August 1920 when a general increase in rates was permitted to offset the continuing higher outgoings.

ADMIRAL with other boats including OWL surrounded by lighters in Regent's Canal Dock. (The Waterways Archive, Gloucester)

: Two pairs of loaded FMC boats head up river through Tower Bridge on the Thames in London en route to Brentford. It is almost certain they had loaded cargoes of sugar at the Tate & Lyle refinery at Silvertown for delivery to businesses in the Birmingham area. (Author's collection)

A significant development that had taken place during the war had been the start of the conversion of the company's fleet of steamers to motor boats. With their restricted cargo space and high crew numbers FMC had investigated ways to improve the position and in November 1906 VULCAN had emerged from Saltley fitted not with a steam engine but with a suction gas engine supplied by Crossleys of Manchester. At about the same time John I Thornycroft & Co. Ltd., which had a marine works at Reading, had acquired DUCHESS and had fitted her up with a 30hp gas engine, the engine room being 3-feet shorter enabling the pay load to be increased to 20 tons. DUCHESS undertook a trial run leaving Brentford on 3 January 1906, arriving in Birmingham a week later and other trips followed. Whilst crew numbers and fuel consumption were reduced, the experiment was not entirely successful and DUCHESS was sold to John Griffiths of Bedworth in 1907 and renamed ANT, whilst FMC converted VULCAN converted

CACTUS was the company's one hundredth motor boat and she is known here at Fazeley Street with a plaque on her cabin side to record the fact. (William Knibbs)

to a conventional steamer in November 1910.

In February 1915 and although her steam engine and boiler were in good condition BARON was fitted up with a model E Bolinder, the conversion work costing £244. BARONESS followed in May except that she was renamed BRITON as the steamers with feminine names were unpopular with the boatmen. EMPEROR was converted in April 1917 the cost of the E-type Bolinder being £162 and the conversion costs having risen to £450. Then EMPRESS was converted at the end of 1919, the work costing £600, a second-hand Bolinder being fitted costing £225 and the boat being renamed ENVOY.

Further conversions had to be deferred, as there was a shortage of new Bolinder engines. So much so that in November 1921 HECLA's machinery was re-assembled in a new wooden hull

at Uxbridge dock; the work was completed in August 1922 at a cost of £635. Uxbridge went on to assemble some old steam machinery in another new wooden hull and DUTEOUS was completed in March 1923 at £720.

The supply of Bolinders improved in 1924 when the decision was taken to convert most of the remaining steamers still in service. GENERAL and SULTAN were dealt with in May but were fitted with the improved Model NE Bolinder which cost £221. Another six were converted before the end of that year, five more followed in 1925, two in 1926 including VANGUARD fitted with a Model BM Bolinder and the remaining three in 1927. The last to be converted was VICEROY, which with Bill Knibbs in charge loaded at City Road Basin and on 6 December 1927 made her final steamer run to Uxbridge where her cargo was transhipped and

she was fitted with a Bolinder.

DUTEOUS and HECLA were the only two wooden steamers that were converted to motors. Of the others EARL was sold in November 1925 for £50 to Charles Court of Stockley, Middlesex who continued to use her widely on the midland canals for several years until her hull gave out and she sank in the gauging lock at Brinklow on the Oxford Canal in February 1937. She was raised and towed to the Brinklow arm and there abandoned but her engine and boiler were taken to Hillmorton maintenance depot and eventually sold for scrap. Meanwhile PIRATE was sold to the Thames Conservancy in December 1902.

QUEEN became the coke boat at Uxbridge in the autumn of 1916 and was finally cut up in 1926, VICTORIA's boiler was damaged in December 1918 and the machinery was dismantled and the hull donated to be used for experiments with a motor; DUKE was cut up in June 1923 as her hull was too expensive to repair whilst PHOENIX was dismantled in September 1925 and her hull sold to be cut up. It seems, however, that SPEEDWELL soldiered on being recorded at Berkhamsted in September 1927 and Nottingham in April 1928 but presumably she succumbed shortly afterwards bringing FMC's great steamer age to an end.

Soon after the war steps were initiated to simplify and reduce the company's share capital. On 28 November 1919 an Extraordinary General Meeting was held at the company's offices in Fazeley Street when it was resolved that the issued capital be reduced from £150,000 to £120,000 by repaying the 3,000 £10 preference shares at par. This involved an application to the court to put the resolution into effect and the court required FMC to show that it had no outstanding creditors before agreeing to the request. On 7 April 1920 all FMC's creditors were paid off but at

FMC was by far the largest carrier on the Warwick Canals so it was fitting that its boats OTTER & GRANGE were used to ferry important guests to the opening ceremony of the new locks at Hatton on 30 October 1934. Steerer Ike Hough was in charge of the pair and he, and several FMC directors subsequently attended the formal dinner in the Shire Hall at Warwick. (The Waterways Archive, Gloucester)

A line of FMC boats frozen in on the Grand Union Canal in 1929 near Cartwright's timber yard at Olton. (Mrs N. Worboys)

the same time the court required written consent from the landlords of all the leased properties, as technically they were also creditors. Hence in September 1920 the Regent's Canal & Dock Company, as landlord of the City Road Basin depot, readily gave its consent commenting FMC was in an excellent position and regularly paid all its accounts.

The repayment went ahead and it was decided that a new company should be registered under the same name. Hence on 25 April 1921 Fellows, Morton and Clayton Limited was registered with company number 174384 with an authorised capital of

£150,000 in £1 shares to acquire the business of the original concern and to carry on in Great Britain and elsewhere the business of carriers by canal, railway, land, sea or otherwise. The first directors were Alfred James Ash, Henry Rodolph de Salis, Graham Baron Ash and Charles Frederick Jones who were required to hold 1,000 shares and who shared remuneration of £1,250 divided between them.

Graham Ash was born on 18 August 1889, the son of Alfred James & Emily Hannah Ash, and had lived at Packwood House, Hockley Heath since 1905. He had been appointed to the board of

the original company on 29 January 1914 but at first his attendance at meetings was sporadic, as he had been serving in the war. Charles Jones had served alongside Alfred Ironmonger and took over from him as the company's senior manager. He was a strict disciplinarian and was always immaculately dressed going round in a horse-drawn carriage. He had joined the original board on 29 November 1918 just after the end of the war.

The establishment of the new company seems to have prompted a decision to change the livery on the boats. The original livery was a black cabin side, surrounded by a thin red bead on a white background. The main lettering, which included the company's name, boat's name and fleet number, was in white. Many of the boats included the figures "1396", this being the company's registration number at the Thames Watermen's Hall. The registration details were painted in black on the white background, and sometimes the individual boat's Watermen's Hall details were included. The new livery comprised a red cabin side, surrounded by a narrow yellow bead on a green background. The lettering remained in white but was simplified as the Watermen's Hall details were no longer included, the last FMC boat to be recorded there being RUSSIA on 26 August 1903. Both liveries featured some modest scroll work.

Apart from the three steamer conversions a few motor boats had been built during the war; these included some iron composite craft from Saltley, such as PLOVER fitted with a 15hp model E Bolinder in January 1915 and costing £550 and some wooden craft from Uxbridge such as QUAIL fitted with a 10hp model E Bolinder in July 1916 and costing £450. With the post war shortage of Bolinders only a few motors could be built but Uxbridge produced another six to follow QUAIL.

When the Bolinder supply position improved in the early 1920s Saltley was heavily involved in a major programme of repairs and so towards the end of 1922 a contract was placed with W. J.

FALCON & STONE at the New Warwick Wharf in October 1939. Danny Brace and Thomas Kendall (in the cap) are on the motor whilst Alice Kendall, Thomas's daughter) steers the butty. (Birmingham Evening Mail)

Yarwood & Sons Ltd. of Northwich in Cheshire to build a batch of a dozen iron composite boats to be fitted with the improved model NE Bolinder. The first to be delivered was ADDER on 4 May 1923 and the order was completed when DRAGON was delivered on 23 January 1925. The price for each boat was entered in the company's docking book as £740 but a note book kept by De Salis gives the price as £726 comprising £430 for the hull and installing the engine, £221 for the engine itself, £63 for labour and materials on fitting out the engine room and £12 for final finishing works at Saltley.

The 12 boats were given consecutive fleet numbers ranging from 285 for ADDER to 296 for DRAGON and a further three fleet numbers were reserved albeit they were never used in practice – 297 FORGET ME NOT, 298 GILLEY FLOWER and 299 GUILDER ROSE. There had also been some uncertainty about two of the names as Yarwoods records show that AVIS was originally intended to have been named ALLIGATOR and CRANE was to have been CROCODILE.

It seems Yarwoods work on the cabins was not entirely satisfactory for the next order was for 12 iron composite hulls of which eight were cabined at Saltley and four at Uxbridge. The first hull, which became EAGLE, was delivered on 5 March 1926 and was completed with a model NE Bolinder at Saltley on 24 April at a cost of £750 and ELK, the first FMC motor to be fitted with a model BM Bolinder, followed her in June. The last hull in the batch was delivered on 9 January 1927 and was completed at Uxbridge on 23 May 1927 as JAGUAR. The analysis of cost again differed with the notebook ascribing it at £724 for the batch - £350 for the hull, £186 for the engine, £106 for the engine room and tanks, and £82 for the cabin and painting.

A third order to Yarwoods was for six iron composite craft with KANGAROO being delivered on 3 May 1928 and the batch being completed with OWL on 12 December 1928. They cost £710 each

The horse drawn pair DRAYTON & GLASGOW pictured in one of the Hanwell flight of locks near Brentford with GLASGOW sporting an attractive horse's tail decoration on her rudder post. (Len Beauchamp)

The boat lady gives a cheerful wave as HANWELL passes south under the ornamental bridge in Grove Park, north of Watford, on 9 April 1934. (Birmingham Central Library)

comprising £463 for the hull and installing the engine, £180 for the engine and £67 for the tanks, fittings and painting.

During all this time FMC continued to invest in its fleet of unpowered boats. In August 1921 Saltley produced the iron composite FAZELEY at a cost of £460 followed by FORWARD in July 1922 but these were the last butties to be built there. Meanwhile Rudkin Brothers of Leicester delivered FRANK in July 1915 costing £145 and VIOLET in May 1916 costing £160. In December 1917 five boats were acquired when FMC took over the remains of the once extensive fleet operated by W. & S. Foster (1912) Ltd. of Tipton.

In 1921 an opportunity came for a major expansion when the Shropshire Union Railways and Canal Company, a subsidiary of the London & North Western Railway Company, decided to give up carrying as a result of heavy losses. FMC stepped in and acquired 25 of the Shropshire Union's most modern boats. They came in two batches – 20 in August 1921 costing £4,650 and the remainder in December at £1,050, a total of £5,700.

At the same time FMC acquired the freehold of the Shropshire Union's premises at Crescent Wharf in the centre of Birmingham on the Newhall Branch Canal reputedly for £45,000. Soon after this acquisition FMC's senior officials hired the inspection launch KINGFISHER, boarded it at Autherley Junction and proceeded to Chester where they stayed overnight, returning to Autherley the next day. Their object was to test the route and the locking system and to conduct a general survey prior to the company starting to trade on the Shropshire Union. Hitherto FMC's traffic to the Mersey had almost invariably been by the Staffordshire & Worcestershire and the Trent & Mersey Canals.

A smaller acquisition followed in July 1922 when the three remaining boats owned by brewers S. Allsopp & Sons Ltd of Burton-on-Trent were acquired for £500 with a further £45 being paid for the boats' cloths.

In May 1917 the Uxbridge yard produced AIRE at a cost of £220, the first of a small class of eight boats named after rivers, the last being EVENLODE in March 1922 costing £340. Shortly afterwards Uxbridge started on its well-known class of boats with girl's names with ADA being commissioned in August 1922 costing £220. The class eventually totalled 27 being completed when JOAN was launched in February 1933 as the very last butty to be built for FMC.

With Saltley no longer building butties FMC turned to outside builders. Between November 1925 and May 1931 Lees & Atkins of Polesworth built eight wooden boats all named after counties. The series started with ESSEX, which cost £280 and finished with CORNWALL. Sephton Brothers at Tusses Bridge, near Coventry built DORSET in March 1926 for £260 whilst William Nurser & Sons of Braunston built EMSCOTE in October 1926 for £250, and two iron boats, MADELEY and MALVERN, were built in 1928 at Harris's boatyard at Netherton.

The purchase of these boats from independent yards seems to have provided FMC with a convenient way to rid itself of old craft as it often insisted that if the yards wanted the work several old boats were taken in part exchange. When what had become Nurser Brothers built BASCOTE at Braunston in May 1929 FMC handed over BLACKCOCK, CLENT, CREWE and ROCHDALE in part payment. Likewise when MIDDLESEX was delivered in April 1930 by Lees & Atkins it accepted ELLESMERE, LANCASTER, RADNOR and RUTLAND with a notional value of £7.10/- (£7.50) each in part exchange towards the total amount due and the firm purchased

A family scene aboard FALCON & FORWARD at Fazeley Street. (Len Beauchamp)

GARDENIA & GRETA heading south on 10 October 1948 at Northchurch. (H. C. Casserley)

another 17 older boats from FMC in the next year or so.

FMC was involved in a novel venture soon after the end of the war. In 1916 the Dunlop Rubber Company had started to build a very large tyre factory on what was then the north-eastern rural outskirts of Birmingham at Aston Cross. As production built up transport to Fort Dunlop became an increasing problem as the nearest tram route was 1½ miles away, there was no convenient railway station and buses were unavailable in the numbers required. The site was close to the Birmingham & Fazeley Canal and to transport workers to it FMC instituted a passenger service in April 1919 using LINDOLA, QUAIL and RAVEN all of which were fitted up with 10hp Bolinder engines. Other boats helped out at times but they were all fitted up with electric lighting and hot water heating and carried the Dunlop name on their cabin sides. The original idea for this service came from Graham Ash who was

working for Dunlops at the time.

The workers were picked up from a wharf near Aston station, the 2½-mile journey to the factory with an intermediate stop at Gravelly Hill near the tram terminus taking between 35 and 40 minutes depending on the amount of traffic on the canal. Two boats left Aston at 6.10am, two at 7.15am, one at 8.40am from Gravelly Hill for office staff, two at 2.10pm and a final eastbound run at 10.10pm for the night shift. There was a similar pattern westbound to tie in with the shifts, the last departure being at 11.20pm. The single fare was 1½d from Aston and 1d from Gravelly Hill. This unique service came to an end in May 1920 when the tramway was extended to much nearer Fort Dunlop.

Whilst FMC normally enjoyed good relations with its boatmen there was a major dispute in 1923 when the company proposed to reduce the rates paid to its crews. This was in a national period of

FERN & UPWOOD entering Lock 52 at Northchurch on 10 October 1948. (H. C. Casserley)

deflation and economic hardship following the war and the company having to reduce its carrying rates by 15% in April to match a reduction imposed by the railways. The proposal was to cut 4/- (20p) per round trip from a steamer working between Brentford and Braunston and 10/- (50p) for a steamer and butty and a 4d (1½p) per ton reduction in the tonnage rates paid, an average overall reduction of about 6½%. FMC had already brushed with the Transport and General Workers Union who represented some of the boatmen and a strike was called starting on 10 August 1923. It centred on Braunston where between 50 and 60 of the company's boats were tied up on the approach to the wharf and stretching along the Grand Junction and Oxford Canals.

The management felt the financial position was such that there was no alternative to imposing the reduction and at a meeting with the union on 16 August it rejected arbitration unless the men would resume work and accept the reduction for the time being. Alternatively it offered to make the reduction in two stages and not to impose any further reductions before March 1924 but it also threatened to liquidate the company if no agreement could be reached. At meetings at Braunston and at other depots the boatmen rejected these proposals. A further meeting was held on 21 August involving Alfred Ash, FMC's chairman, and Sir David Shackleton, the chief adviser to the Ministry of Labour, but no progress was made.

Matters were no further forward in October when FMC's solicitors sent letters to all the strikers seeking to evict them from the cabin homes, this being prompted by the company needing to unload the cargoes onto lorries and distribute them to its anxious customers. At Braunston some 1,000 tons of sugar and tea

Grouped around the stern of LAMPREY are Harold Worboys, the superintendent of the Northern fleet where LAMPREY was earmarked to serve), steerer Meredith, Mr. W. Henman (Manager of Saltley Dock where the Yarwoods built hull was fitted out), Mr. Thrasher (Marine Engineer at Saltley Dock) and Arthur Humphries. (Mrs N. Worboys)

destined for Birmingham were involved and after an initial unsuccessful attempt three boats had been successfully unloaded on 5 September with a detachment of police standing by to ensure there were no breaches of the peace.

The eviction threat lingered on and eventually the issue of trespass on the company's boats came to the High Court before Mr. Justice Romer on 9 November. By now both the company and the men were mindful to settle the dispute and the union proposed a return to work at the rates applying before the strike but with arbitration on future rates then to take place. FMC agreed to this proposal as did the men at depot meetings on 18

November and the boats began to move on the following morning. The strike had lasted just over 14 weeks.

Arbitration took place at an industrial court in London on 20 November and decided that the proposed reduction went too far particularly for those on the horse boat traffic where lower rates always applied. Instead an initial reduction of 2½% was to take effect from 19 November with a further 2½% reduction from 19 December. For FMC it was a dark period in its history and whilst no steps were taken to carry out the threatened liquidation, enquiries were made into trying to sell the company, but at that time there were no buyers.

LAMPREY has arrived at Knowle Top Lock after her test run from Sampson Road. The lock side is still cluttered up with materials from the recent widening of the locks here, where six narrow (7-feet) locks were replaced by five wide (14-feet) locks. (Mrs N. Worboys)

On 19 July 1925 Alfred Ash died and Henry Rodolph De Salis took his place as FMC's chairman. Another loss was Frederick Morton who died of old age and heart failure on 12 May 1921 at his home in Southport aged 86 years. Despite his age Morton had been a regular attender at board meetings nearly up to the end, his last being on 30 December 1920. His wife Mary survived him by ten years dying at the Southport home on 14 October 1930 aged 92 years.

To replace him on the board James Henry Clayton was appointed a director on 6 July 1921. He was born on 30 January 1863, the third son of William Clayton, and had worked for FMC for many years, latterly being based in the London area to control operations there. Ash's replacement was Frank Eagleton Fellows who was appointed to the board on 31 March 1926. He was born on 5 March 1871 at West Bromwich, the seventh son of Joshua. Several of Joshua's other sons had been involved with the company – for instance his eldest son, Frederick William, born at Wednesbury in 1860, was employed as depot manager at 30 Canal Street, Nottingham until his early death on 28 August 1896 at the age of 36. His wife, Mary Alice, then went to live at Joshua's home at Woodville, Barnt Green and she inherited the property following the death of her mother-in-law in 1902. And after FMC was formed, Joshua's brother James, who had been a partner in Fellows Morton, became an agent with the Severn & Canal Carrying Company until his death in 1905.

CHAPTER SIX
OPERATIONS AND TRAFFICS

Latterly FMC's boats worked in two fleets - the Southern Fleet based on the Grand Union Canal between London, Birmingham and Nottingham and the Northern Fleet working between Wolverhampton, Ellesmere Port, Liverpool, Manchester and Nottingham. Sometimes if there was a rush of traffic boats would have to be diverted. The southern boatmen disliked this as it meant a drop in earnings for only 45 tons could be carried on a pair on the Shropshire Union Canal owing to the lack of depth in the channel compared to at least 54 tons on the Grand Union.

For a time six pairs were based at Nottingham and were known as the Nottingham Fleet but later they became part of the Northern Fleet. Flour from Sun Mills, goods from Brown & Poulson and newsprint were regular traffics from Manchester to Nottingham. Problems arose in 1925 when Rugeley viaduct carrying the railway line over the canal collapsed closing the Trent & Mersey Canal for 16 weeks. Horses and drays had to be used between Rugeley wharf and Handsacre with transhipping at both ends. A short-lived traffic in the Nottingham area was to carry sugar beet to a processing factory, which had opened in 1924 beside the river Trent at Colwick but the carriage of sugar from the factory lasted much longer, one important contract being to supply to Cadburys' factory at Knighton on the Shropshire Union Canal.

The horses used between Norton Junction and Nottingham had to be specially selected as the route involved a considerable mileage of river work. When returning from Nottingham strength was needed to tow a loaded boat up the Trent against the current on the Five Mile Pound, known as the Cranfleet Cut. Intelligence was also needed when towing boats downstream for the towpath often formed part of the adjoining fields and the horse had to push open swing gates without stopping so as to prevent the boat losing

LYNX and its butty leave Batchworth Lock No 81 on 14 July 1928 whilst another pair waits above. (Hertfordshire County Council)

Directors and officers of the company take lunch aboard the inspection launch KINGFISHER in 1922 whilst on their tour of inspection of the Shropshire Union Canal. Left to right the group comprises William Bradshaw, (Superintendent of the Northern fleet), John Ironmonger (Director and Secretary), William Henry Jones (Chief of the office staff), William Anderson (Superintendent of the Southern fleet), Henry Rodolph De Sales (Director) and Charles Frederick Jones (Managing Director). (Author's collection)

steerage way. Going down the Trent the horse often had to move at a trot all the time.

To get a butty across from the river Soar to the Cranfleet Cut or the Erewash Canal a 285-feet towing line would be used. From the actual junction the horse towed as hard as possible along the south bank of the Trent until it was well upstream of the two entrances opposite. The line was then cast off and the momentum together with the opposing current of the Trent slanted the boat across to where it needed to go. The boat crew had to haul in the towing line very quickly as otherwise it would act as an anchor. The horse then went on up river and crossed on the ferry. The Trent here could be shallow and there was a great danger the boat could run aground or get out of control in the swift current. DRAYTON and SOMERSET were once swept downstream over Thrumpton weir and were stranded for a week.

When a boat wanted to cross over to the Soar the 285-feet line

Violet and Dolly Beechey standing on ROBIN's cabin from which they escaped unhurt after an enemy bomb had fallen and badly damaged and sank two loaded pairs at the New Warwick Wharf on 1 November 1940. ROBIN & KILDARE on the left were carrying tubes from Coombeswood to London whilst ROVER & GRACE were loaded with cocoa for Manchester. (Birmingham Evening Mail)

was attached to the horse with the other end secured near to the boat. The horse then went up river to cross over to the south bank of the Trent on the ferry, still with the line attached. Once the horse was in position, the line was attached to the boat, which then cast off and was towed into the Soar where the horse stopped so that the long line could be shortened for the normal line, which for the Soar was 135-feet. There were wooden posts up the Soar towpath to guide the horses in times of flood when the water could get up to the horses' bellies. A motor boat could not operate under these conditions, the guide posts being of no help to it.

FMC was probably one of the last traders to use the Derby Canal. It had operated steamer services to the town from London,

Nottingham and Birmingham for many years, sugar being the most important traffic; others included grain, flour, wood pulp and china clay. One return traffic was pipes from Stantons ironworks, which passed through the canal en route to Birmingham at least until 1930. FMC's agent was John William Gandy who occupied a rented warehouse at Derby's Morledge wharf. Gandy had been one of the initial shareholders in FMC and he also operated as a carrier and had a virtual monopoly of the trade between Derby and Preston Brook. When he gave up carrying in 1917 FMC took over the Morledge warehouse for a while. Following this FMC brought in occasional cargoes from the north-west such as a consignment of sugar from Liverpool in February 1931. In 1926 107 boats brought 1,906 tons, mainly sugar and tinned goods from London to Derby whilst 27 boats took 588 tons of pipes through the canal from Stantons.

By this time the Derby Canal was in poor condition, loadings were restricted and the canal company was considering possible closure moves. It is believed the last FMC boat to traverse the entire length of the canal from Sandiacre via Derby to Swarkestone was on 20 February 1935 when captain Smith took 4¾ tons of sugar to Derby and 5 cwt of empty drums to Swarkestone. On 2 March 1936 captain Bob Gopsill's boat took 7¾ tons of general goods from Derby to Sandiacre and again it is thought this was the last FMC boat to use this section of the canal. FMC's last traffic was from Swarkestone to Derby in November 1938 but by that time most of the company's trade to and from the town was handled by road.

The normal load for a pair of "joshers", as FMC's ordinary carrying boats were known in affectionate memory of Joshua Fellows, was 23 tons on the motor and 27 tons on the butty but this was by no means an absolute maximum. In February 1926 HECLA loaded 26 tons and FAZELEY 29 tons of iron tubes from Coombs Wood, near Halesowen for delivery to Brentford, making 55 tons for the pair. With this load the boats can have had hardly any freeboard - it used to be said that sparrows could sometimes sit on the gunwale and drink water from the canal and the boatmen often referred to such boats as "sparrow-drinkers".

All joshers tended to dig in at the fore-end when going hard – heavily laden motors sometimes had water up the cratch when going across places like Leighton Wide on the Grand Union Canal. Many captains used to shut the foredeck lid over a piece of tarpaulin to keep it watertight but one, going hard up the Trent, had neglected to do this and rather than slow down he had to stand up front on the top plank holding the cover down with a mop. On 27 April 1927 SWALLOW & VERBENA were going fast through Blisworth tunnel at night to try and reach Long Buckby

An FMC pair has just entered Ironbridge Lock No 77 at Watford on 19 June 1937.
(Hertfordshire County Council)

The horse drawn pair JAMES & VERBENA head south through Watford's Cassiobury Park on 29 July 1928. (Hertfordshire County Council)

before a stoppage. Water washed over into VERBENA's foredeck, lifted a loose lid, flooded the foredeck and the boat nose-dived with 27½ tons of sugar on board. The tunnel had to be drained to refloat her.

Apart from the fly boat services, which ran until the outbreak of the Second World War when air raid precautions involving the installation of stop planks at night made their operation impractical, even the ordinary joshers had to keep to a schedule. Five days were allowed for a typical journey from London to Birmingham although many boatmen reckoned to do it in four. Before starting a boatman would receive a payment on account, "starting money", which was about £5 in the 1930s. The balance was paid when the trip was completed. Extra payments were made if the crews had to load or unload the cargo or if extra speed was called for, requiring night working.

Sometimes lorries were used to speed up an urgent consignment as, for instance in 1931 when PYTHON & DART broke down just above the City Road locks on the Regent's Canal. Part of DART's cargo was 8½ tons of tea destined for 28 shops in Coventry.

Once repaired, the boats reached Braunston in 39½ hours where they were met by lorries sent from Birmingham, which collected the tea and delivered it to the shops on time.

This was a special arrangement as the joshers were by no means slow. De Salis noted that in November 1927 ADMIRAL & UPTON, captained by Tom Green, had left Nottingham empty and arrived at Stewarts & Lloyds, Coombs Wood, in 33 hours – 75 miles via Farmers Bridge and 60 locks most of which were narrow and so had to be worked twice. They loaded with tubes, stayed overnight at Fazeley Street, and then did the trip to Brentford in just over 72 hours – 149 miles and 159 locks of which 58 had to be worked twice.

ADMIRAL & PORTUGAL, this time captained by Joseph Green, featured in another fast run in June 1930 when after discharging ore at Coombs Wood and reloading with tubes they reached Brentford in well under three days enabling their cargo to be alongside the export steamer a day later. In 1934 when FMC was competing with the Great Western Railway for a 300-ton order, CLOVER & KILBURN delivered 47 tons of oil pipes from Coombs

Wood to the Royal Albert Dock in such a fast time that the pipes had been in the ship's hold for four hours before the railway wagons arrived. With the greatly reduced maintenance standards of the canals after the First World War these were creditable performances. Both Northern and Southern fleets visited Coombs Wood with five or six pairs taking away tubes every week.

The Northern boatmen had to contend with special problems when working a pair on the Shropshire Union. A long line – five 90-feet lines joined together – would be used coming up Hack Green, Audlem, Adderley and Tyrley locks so that the motor, albeit a lock ahead, could still tow the butty. This technique needed good teamwork with the butty steerer signalling when the butty had reached the lock, the final pulling in being done by hand. By this means a pair could be worked two-handed with the butty's tiller being held in position with strings.

Long lines did not work going downhill and the butty had to be bowhauled. Fortunately the boats usually were empty working northwards on the Shroppie. Long lines were sometimes used at Hatton, before the lock widenings, and at Atherstone. The company had a stable at the top of the Wolverhampton flight of 21 locks as a long line was of no use there. Southbound boatmen used to despatch a crew member by bicycle or bus from Brewood to harness up a horse and get it down to the bottom of the flight ready for the boats to arrive. Sometimes plans went wrong; one boatman having to chase two horses at a gallop down the locks on his bike.

Most Northern length boats unloaded at Albion Wharf, Wolverhampton but some went through to Birmingham to unload at either Crescent Wharf or Baskerville Basin, both of which were at the top of the Farmers Bridge flight of locks in the centre of the city, and later Sherborne Street Wharf. The Northern boatmen were reputed to dislike the Farmers Bridge locks and rarely

BRITON & NORTHOLT at Trent Lock with their skipper Dick Humphries (partly enveloped in smoke) and his wife. The Humphries were on the London to Nottingham run until 1936 when they left to live at Braunston. (Ike Argent)

ventured down them to access the Fazeley Street wharves. The main destination for the Southern boats was Fazeley Street and at times there were so many boats unloading or waiting to unload that it was almost impossible for other boats to get by.

FMC carried almost every type of cargo imaginable. At one time turpentine in barrels was an important traffic from London to Birmingham but boats loaded with this cargo had to carry a red warning light and they were never allowed to tie up near any built-up area.

In the 1920s sugar accounted for no less than 40% of all traffic handled. It was carried from both London and Liverpool for all the leading manufacturers in the midlands usually in 1cwt or 2cwt sacks although preserving sugar came in 3cwt sacks. The company had a near monopoly supplying shops and factories within a four-mile radius of Birmingham. Much of the sugar brought from Liverpool was destined for Cadburys' processing factory at Knighton.

Tea was also handled in large quantities with the company again supplying most shops in Birmingham. Here 228 cases comprised a "blend of tea", which weighed just over 15 tons and just fitted onto a motor boat. Typhoo Tea Ltd. had a wharf at Bordesley Street close to FMC's Warwick Wharf. One boat used to leave City Road every Friday night carrying 16 tons of groceries for the Maypole shops in Birmingham - it was known as the Maypole boat.

Another important traffic was in metals, particularly from the Regent's Canal Dock at Limehouse to Birmingham and from Manchester docks to Wolverhampton, Dudley Port and Crescent Wharf. This traffic was not without hazards; once WINSFORD was being loaded at Manchester when she tipped, the metal slid, and the boat rolled over and sank. A diver was sent down immediately but not to start salvaging the cargo. Hidden in a mattress were 100 gold sovereigns, the life savings of the elderly steerer, and the diver's first task was to recover them. Copper in

Mrs Emma Russon sits at the stern of BASCOTE at Hatton Locks in 1935. (Walter Russon)

HAWK & HETTIE head north from Shrewley Tunnel in July 1955, (Jack Parkinson)

4cwt ingots was brought from Nottingham for the Birmingham Battery Company at Selly Oak near the east end of the Lapal tunnel.

An important traffic for the Northern fleet was bagged flour from Ellesmere Port to Wolverhampton and Bloxwich. When loading the bags came down a chute in a continual stream and required rapid stacking.

Other traffics included cocoa beans from Nottingham to Bournville, grain, coal, iron and steel, chemicals, rubber, fire bricks, cement. cheese, canned goods, dates and figs, fruit, vegetable pulp, earthenware goods, and timber. At Fazeley Street an arm of the canal was known as "The Bedstead Hole" where thousands of iron bedsteads were loaded for London for export to the world. One of the regular chemical traffics was acid in glass-lined barrels from Chance & Hunt Ltd. at Oldbury and taken up Bow Creek to West Ham.

During the Second World War one pair used to leave Wednesbury every day and work to Purfleet on the Thames loaded with anti-aircraft shell cases. They usually worked with all-male crews like flyboats and ADMIRAL & GREECE often operated together on this run.

At one time FMC boats used to work down the river Nene regularly to Whitworth's mill at Wellingborough and to Trenery's timber yard there. They occasionally also went right down to

An unidentified pair passing southwards through Slapton Bridge No 120 on the Grand Union Canal in the 1930s. (The Waterways Archive, Gloucester)

Peterborough but the Nene was not an easy river and required good boating skills and a reliable horse. Another traffic on this river was to transport railway chairs from Oundle. For many years Northampton was served by a regular market boat and when a butty was involved a horse took it through the Rothersthorpe locks, a practice that was continued well into the 1960s by the company's successors. Market boats also served both Uxbridge and Aylesbury for a while.

The company made regular journeys to Stratford-upon-Avon originally seeming to share the traffic with the Severn & Canal Company. From the 1920s FMC had a virtual monopoly of traffic on this canal using mainly horse drawn singles or pairs. One of the last boats to reach the town was KESWICK captained by J. Nightingale in January 1935 but the canal became virtually impassable soon afterwards.

FMC also had some traffic on the Stourbridge Canal and for a few years from 1900 advertised a regular service to the north-west. For many years an important traffic was in firebricks, which were taken down to London. This ceased probably in the early 1930s bringing the company's trade on the Stourbridge to a temporary halt. In 1938 FMC carried a few cargoes of firebricks

from E. J. & J. Pearson at the Delph to the Potteries on behalf of the Anderton Company and it took over the entire traffic in 1941. On 9 May 1941 two boats loaded 42 tons of firebricks at Brettell Lane, Stourbridge and subsequently other cargoes followed such as cement and bran.

In the Second World War the Ministry of Supply started storing aluminium at Amblecote near Stourbridge and FMC delivered some of the metal, the first two boats arriving from Liverpool on 28 May 1943 with 34 tons. By early in 1945 three pairs a week were delivering with FMC handling all the metal from Liverpool and the Grand Union Canal Carrying Co. Ltd. that from Aylesbury and Slough, but with help from FMC. When the traffic started the canal was in poor condition and payloads were restricted; the first two boats carried only 17 tons each but still experienced difficulties. By early 1945 matters had improved and FMC pairs were passing with 44 to 45 tons without any trouble.

To provide a backload for the London boats the company had tried to revive the firebrick traffic from Pearsons at the Delph but could not compete against rates quoted by the railway. However the company carried shells from the naval depot at Nagersfield, part way down the Stourbridge flight of locks, to London and hand grenades were loaded at Brettell Lane for both London and Manchester.

In January 1947 the Ministry of Supply started to disperse the aluminium stockpile, FMC refusing 400 tons from Amblecote to Banbury but in June a pair loaded for Ponders End on the river Lee and three pairs for Warrington. A month later 195 tons were sent to Ponders End.

The company's main stables were at Liverpool Street in Birmingham where separate accommodation was provided for the boat and the dray horses. Stables were also maintained at City Road, Long Buckby, Braunston, Nottingham, Wolverhampton, Great Heywood, Preston Brook and Audlem. Those at Great Haywood and Long Buckby ceased to be used in 1930 and Braunston followed in 1934 but horses were still used at the Camp Hill and Wolverhampton locks at least until the end of 1948. FMC's horses were all numbered on the right hoof.

Warehousing played an important part of the undertaking. In Birmingham the company had a series of wharves – Warwick Wharf, Fazeley Street, Crescent Wharf and Sherborne Street – where large amounts of various commodities could be stored against the fluctuating needs of many customers. For instance 10 tons of newsprint had to be delivered each day to the Birmingham Post & Mail, as did 20 tons of sultanas and 20 tons of sugar to Scribbans, the cake and biscuit manufacturers. There were also warehouses at Wolverhampton, Dudley Port, Leicester, Nottingham, Brentford, City Road, Northampton and other centres.

In the 1920s and having previously relied on outside haulage firms, the company started to build up a fleet of lorries to provide an efficient delivery and collection service from and to its depots. In the early 1930s the company had two Foden steam lorries, two Albion 4-tonners, a Leyland six-wheeler, a Scammel tractor unit with several trailers, a fleet of smaller Ford trucks and vans, and a large number of horse-drawn carts most of which were based in

CLOVER & KESWICK leaving Stoke Hammond Lock No 23 on the Grand Union Canal on their way northwards in about 1936. (The Waterways Archive, Gloucester)

Albert & Emma Russon, who had the pair BRAMBLE & BASCOTE, outside the Six Bells public house in Brentford with the lockkeeper from Thames Lock No 101 smoking his pipe. A friend and the lock keeper's wife stand behind. (Walter Russon)

the Birmingham area.

The Foden steam lorries were used to collect casks of beer from Mitchells & Butler's Cape Hill Brewery for loading at Fazeley Street and subsequent delivery to a bonded warehouse at Park Royal on the Paddington branch with the empties making up a return loading. The Albions were used to deliver glucose and sugar to the Black Country sugar boilers, for miscellaneous traffic from Brentford and the City Road Basin, and for delivering borax to Dudley Port for fluxing in the enamel trade and aluminium for cooking utensils. The Ford vehicles handled smaller deliveries such as canned milk, tinned fruits and meats, lime juice, marmalade, honey, castor and granulated sugar and tea to every multiple store throughout Birmingham including Home & Colonial, Meadow Dairy, Wrensons, George Mason, the Birmingham Coop and Lyons Restaurants.

In 1948 the company had 15 vehicles based at Birmingham including a Scammel with two trailers, two Dennis lorries, four Ford lorries, six Morris Commercials and two vans. The majority of these were fairly new having been acquired since 1945 but a few dated back to 1937. Other vehicles were based at City Road, Wolverhampton and Nottingham together with three at Uxbridge for the coal business. Except for those at Uxbridge and one of the vans all of them had the-then obligatory "A" licences entitling them to operate freely in and around Birmingham.

For many years William Anderson, known universally as Mac Anderson but always addressed as Mr. Anderson, had been in charge of the Southern Fleet. He was respected as being strict but fair and he always knew where each boat should be and sometimes went out to check up. Woe betide any boatman he found tied up when he should have been moving, but when he found the boat on time or ahead of schedule he would often give the boatman a pound note to buy a round of drinks that night. He

Standing on the counter of the motor LAPWING the Grand Junction Canal's toll clerk uses his gauging rod to measure the freeboard on butty KILBURN. By this means the weight of the cargo, and hence the toll payable, could be assessed from tables kept at the nearby toll office. (The Waterways Archive, Gloucester)

BRAMBLE & BASCOTE entering the south end of Shrewley Tunnel with Albert & Emma Russon, on the stern of the butty in about 1935. (Walter Russon)

kept a strict control on the amount of fuel used and if the allowance was exceeded the boatman would be called into the office and if there was no satisfactory explanation he would be dismissed. Mac Anderson died in 1942 with Leslie Painter taking his place.

Meanwhile William Samuel Bradshaw had been in charge of the Northern Fleet for many years until he shot himself in 1932. Harold Brooks Worboys, who had joined FMC in 1904, took his place and served until his retirement in March 1949.

CHAPTER SEVEN
THE FINAL FLING

Throughout the 1930s the company continued to invest in its motor boat fleet. A fourth order went to Yarwoods in February 1929 introducing a new feature for when PANTHER was delivered to Saltley for fitting out in October 1929, followed a month later by

PYTHON, both had hulls of coppered-steel plates. They were commissioned in February 1930 and fitted with model BM Bolinders, the hulls costing £366 and the engines £180 each. A fifth order followed in December 1930 for three similar hulls costing £355 each, the first, ACACIA, being commissioned in July 1931.

The sixth Yarwood order, made on 12 July 1932, introduced another new feature being the first motor boat designed to work as a single unit, without a butty. The coppered-steel hull for what became BREAM arrived at Saltley on 15 December 1932 at a cost of £340. A 12hp Bolinder reduced to 9hp had been ordered from Pollocks of Faversham on 30 July 1932 at a cost of £116.25. BREAM's shaft was fitted 2 inches lower than for a more normal 15hp motor and her stowage was 47ft 8in compared to 45ft 6in for a 15hp motor or 50ft 6in for a horse boat.

BREAM underwent a trial on 14 February 1933 from Sampson

Road Wharf to Knowle top lock carrying 20¼ tons with 12 inches of dry side during which her engine was tested up to 560 revolutions per minute, which was considerably higher than FMC's normal practice. Subsequently she was loaded up to 25 tons, which gave 7 inches of dry side. She cost £660 in all and was the forerunner of the fish class of boats of which the company had another 17 built over the next 3½ years. Yarwoods built all but two of the hulls; three had similar coppered-steel hulls to BREAM but the final 12 were of iron composite construction. The two exceptions were BRILL and CARP, which were built at Uxbridge with wooden hulls.

These single motors were used by the company on the narrow locked Shropshire Union and Trent & Mersey Canals to avoid the delays caused by double lockage for a normal motor and butty.

The seventh batch from Yarwoods comprised five craft with either coppered steel or iron composite hulls. The first, BRAMBLE, was completed at Northwich on 16 April 1934 and after fitting out at Uxbridge entered service at the end of July. One of this batch - CACTUS - had the distinction of being FMC's one-hundredth motor boat and carried a commemorative plaque on her cabin side to record this. She entered service in May 1935 at a cost of £750.

Yarwoods next contract was work on the hulls of a series of 12 iron composite butties as a prelude to converting them into single motors - the first to be re-commissioned, after finishing work at Saltley, was FRANCE in May 1937. She had been built with a fore cabin at Saltley in August 1904 but this was removed as part of the conversion and she was fitted with a 9hp Bolinder. Seven others also had fore cabins, which were similarly removed. The batch was completed when COLUMBIA was reconditioned in January 1939.

Meanwhile Uxbridge had continued to produce a few new wooden motors and had also cabined some of the Yarwood hulls. ASTER was launched with a 15hp model BM Bolinder in June 1932 at a cost of £560 to be followed three months later by AZALEA.

Mrs Martha Humphries on FREDA in April 1940. (Robert May Collection)

Under the awning at the New Warwick Wharf in October 1940 with Billy & Hilda Harrison on the motor boat LAUREL talking to Jim Webb on the motor CLOVER whilst George Brookes peers out of CLOVER's engine room and Ike Argent is dealing with cartons of H.P. sauce on the extreme right. (Birmingham Evening Mail)

The two Fish class motors followed, BRILL costing £500 and CARP £515, which was considerably less than the metal-hulled craft. In January 1935 BEGONIA, the first of a batch of six wooden motors was launched, the last being ERICA in February 1937.

From the autumn of 1929 the company had started replacing the early model E Bolinder engines with the improved model BM engine. Twenty-three boats had model E engines fitted and the first to be converted was LEOPARD in September 1929 at Saltley followed by BRITON at Uxbridge in January 1930, the replacement engines costing £180. The work was completed in May 1935 when RAMBLER was converted at Saltley.

With FMC's policy of keeping its fleet up to date it was always seeking buyers to take some of its older craft. In the early years an important customer for such boats was the Union Acid Co. Ltd of Manchester, which took 30 mainly between 1899 and 1915. The boat builders Lees & Atkins of Polesworth and Nursers of Braunston each took 20 boats but the largest purchaser was Ernest Thomas of Walsall who took over 40 craft between 1941 and 1948 including many of the former steamers. Between 1929 and 1932 another notable purchaser was the Grand Union Canal Company, which used the boats in connection with improvements it was carrying out to its waterway.

There were many smaller buyers such as A. J. Harmsworth & Son of Aldershot, the Boots Pure Drug Co. Ltd of Nottingham, Cadbury Brothers Ltd of Bournville, the Erewash Canal Company, W. H. Green of Stoke-on-Trent, Imperial Chemical Industries Ltd of Oldbury, J. B. Price of Burslem, the Manchester Ship Canal Company, the Oxford Canal Company, Samuel Barlow Coal Co. Ltd. of Birmingham and Smith Stone & Knight Ltd. of Birmingham who all acquired four or more boats each and there were large numbers of smaller buyers.

On 6 October 1934 Uxbridge launched PIONEER, a new wide motor boat designed to operate on the inter-mill traffic for John Dickinson & Co. Ltd. with two less crew than a pair of narrow boats.

GARDENIA & GRETA with Tom Humphries in charge southbound light at bridge 183 below Denham Deep Lock in June 1954. (Topical Press)

The view looking towards Wolverhampton Top Basin and near to Albion Wharf showing FMC boats iced in during the winter of 1929. (Mrs N. Worboys)

NORTHWICH loaded with 25 tons of cocoa from Cadburys heads northwards at Audlem on the Shropshire Union Canal in the 1940s with Mrs Leah Tolley in charge of the horse. FMC served the Cadbury Brothers factories at both Bournville and Knighton dealing with cocoa beans, chocolate crumb and mass, the finished products and cocoa residue that was exported. (Mrs Rose Gibbs, Leah Tolley's daughter)

Her first trial run was from the boatyard through Cowley lock to the Great Western Railway bridge at Hayes, a distance of just over 5 miles in 94 minutes including the one lock giving an average speed of 3¼ mph. Her second trial was an operational one on 29 November from Apsley mill calling at Nash, Home Park and Croxley mills with an overnight stop at Uxbridge before delivering to Dickinsons' Kings Cross depot at midday on the following day. After discharging and reloading she stopped for the weekend at Uxbridge and discharged at Nash Mill on Monday afternoon. Although she could carry up to 66 tons it was found in practice she could not maintain the tight schedule demanded by Dickinsons and she was sold to the Harefield Lime Co. Ltd early in 1936.

One of the major developments that affected FMC in the 1930s was the Grand Union Canal Company's decision to widen the narrow locks on the Warwick Canals with the aim of introducing wide-beam craft onto the route. With the help of a government subsidy on the interest on part of the borrowed money the Grand Union replaced the 52 narrow locks between Calcutt and Sampson Road with 51 wide ones. At the same time several bridges were rebuilt with spans that did not restrict the waterway, many miles of concrete bank protection were installed and much dredging work was carried out. Restrictions on finance meant that the scheme could not be completed and whilst trials were made with a wide-beam motor boat, traffic on this section continued to be handled by narrow boats.

For FMC, however, there was a major benefit as the transhipment work at Braunston could now be eliminated and the use of horses on this section could be dispensed with, giving the company annual savings of between £2,500 and £3,000 in costs and reductions in transit times.

The formal opening of the widened locks took place at Hatton on 30 October 1934 when the company's boats OTTER & GRANGE,

The motor boat EAGLE on the Shropshire Union Canal in the 1940s with Alf Whalley in charge. Until 1921 FMC hardly ever used the Shropshire Union with traffic to and from Manchester and the northwest always travelling via the Trent & Mersey Canal. (Jack Whalley)

suitably fitted up with awnings, transported some of the invited guests to the ceremony. Afterwards there was a dinner in the Shire Hall at Warwick, which was attended by Rodolph de Salis and John Ironmonger on behalf of FMC's directors, several of the senior staff and Ike Hough, OTTER's steerer.

On 24 June 1935 the Grand Union Canal Company granted FMC a 99-year lease for Warwick Wharf at Fazeley Street and on 19 August construction work began on a large new warehouse building at the entrance to the basin. This was completed in the following year but on 16 November 1938 FMC purchased the freehold from the Grand Union for £17,500. Another development in 1935 was the company starting to use Sherborne Street Wharf on the Oozells Street loop line off the Birmingham Canal's main line. This was due to the impending loss of the company's Crescent Wharf whose site was involved in the City of Birmingham's Civic Centre reconstruction scheme. Crescent

Wharf was ultimately disposed of for £53,000 with FMC investing in a substantial new warehouse at Sherborne Street to replace the lost facility. The Birmingham Canal Navigations dredged considerable parts of the loop to accommodate traffic to the new warehouse, which opened in 1938.

Another development was on 1 July 1938 when the fleet of Midlands & Coast Canal Carriers Ltd., which was based at Wolverhampton, was acquired. Midlands & Coast had been established by Noah Hingley & Sons Ltd. of Netherton Ironworks on 1 April 1922 to take the place of the Shropshire Union fleet on which it had depended heavily. Before doing so an approach had been made to FMC to provide an export service to Ellesmere Port but initially the company had declined, prompting Hingleys to act to protect itself from being totally dependent on the railways. Nearly 30 of the Shropshire Union's wooden boats were acquired but later some new steel boats were built for the company by

John Crichton & Co. Ltd. at its Saltney yard on the river Dee near Chester and by Yarwoods at Northwich on the river Weaver. The company traded mainly on the Shropshire Union but there was also some traffic on the Grand Junction down to London, two of the company's boats, JUPITER & MARS, featuring at Braunston in the 1923 boatmen's strike.

Midlands & Coast was based at Broad Street depot in Wolverhampton, which was held on a sub-lease dated 30 November 1922 from the London & North Western Railway Company; in turn the railway had taken a 99-year lease from the Birmingham Canal Navigations in 1869. Midlands & Coast's initial rent was £300 but this was progressively reduced owing to trading difficulties faced by the company and by the time FMC took over it was down to £100. In 1924 Henry Roger Holder had been appointed manager and after the take-over he remained as assistant manager at Wolverhampton. Four motor boats and 12 butties were involved and most were disposed of by FMC over the next few years.

The outbreak of the Second World War on 1 September 1939 soon had a similar adverse effect as the 1914 war. Wages and prices rose but the government imposed tight control on all carrying rates preventing the company recouping its losses. As an interim measure the Ministry of Transport started paying FMC and other carriers a subsidy of 50% of the canal tolls incurred from 1 June 1940. This was followed by the Ministry assuming control of FMC from 1 July 1942 and under a financial agreement dated 12 October 1944 the company was relieved of all carrying losses and in addition was to receive a guaranteed income, which was sufficient to pay the shareholders a dividend of 6%.

During all this time there were a series of changes to the company's directors and staff. On 17 October 1930 the managing director, Charles Frederick Jones, died after a lifetime of service with FMC culminating in being appointed to the board in 1918. One of his achievements was the setting up of a Superannuation

Skipper Joe Tolley on the motor boat DRAGON at Ellesmere Port during the 1940s. (Mrs Rose Gibbs, daughter of Mrs Leah Tolley)

The butty ENA entering Dudswell Bottom Lock No 48 on the Grand Union Canal on her way north on 6 July 1935. (Hertfordshire County Council)

Fund for the benefit of staff on retirement; a Trust Deed dated 1 June 1927 under which the Midland Bank was appointed trustee governed it. John Ironmonger, the son of Alfred, was now appointed managing director and he joined the board on 7 November 1930. He had been born on 26 October 1872, had joined the company on 2 June 1890 and had worked his way up conscientiously, taking over as secretary from his father. His son, Ralph, now took on the role of company secretary.

On 1 July 1935 Frank Eagleton Fellows resigned as a director owing to ill health and his place was taken by Edward Bosley, an accountant. Then on 25 February 1936 De Salis, who had been in poor health for some time, committed suicide. He was 69 years old and had been a director for nearly 39 years including nearly 11 years as chairman. His funeral took place at Old Milverton Church, Leamington, near to his home, on 29 February.

To replace De Salis James Henry Clayton took over as chairman, serving until 29 September 1939, whilst Colonel Forrester Clayton was appointed a director on 7 May 1936. Forrester had been born on 3 November 1878 and became an Alderman for the County of Middlesex and a Justice of the Peace. He lived at Brentford from where he oversaw FMC's operations at the southern end of the Grand Union Canal and he was also served as managing director of Thomas Clayton (Oldbury) Ltd. hence continuing FMC's links with that concern. He took over from James Clayton as FMC's chairman in 1939.

Forrester Clayton died on 6 August 1942 aged 63 and John Ironmonger then took on the dual role of chairman and managing director. On 9 October 1942 three additional directors were appointed - William Henry Jones, Ralph Hall Ironmonger and William Blyth Clayton. Jones, always known as Mr Henry, was chief

The motor boat LYNX and her butty leave Black Jack's Lock No 85 at Harefield on the way south on 14 July 1928. The house on the right was at one time lived in by Charles Alexander Mercer, who served the Grand Junction Canal Company for over 40 years, ending up as company secretary. (Hertfordshire County Council)

of the office staff at Fazeley Street; Ralph Ironmonger, John's son, had been involved with the company since about 1920; whilst William Clayton was James Henry's son.

The ending of the Second World War on 2 September 1945 gave little respite for the company, which remained firmly under government control. During the war it had not been possible for any new boats to join the fleet although three motor boats had been rebuilt with new wooden hulls at Uxbridge in 1940 and 1941. But in September 1946 Uxbridge launched the motor boat CHILTERN at a cost of £900. She was fitted with a 9hp Bolinder and was the first of a new Hill class intended to work in the company's northern fleet based on Wolverhampton. She was followed in June 1947 by CLEE costing £972 and in December by CLENT costing £1,080, all these prices reflecting wartime inflation.

Meanwhile an order had been placed with Yarwoods for six coppered-steel hulls and the first became FERN in June 1947. She was fitted out at Saltley with a 15hp model BM Bolinder and cost £1,650; the second, FOXGLOVE, followed in December.

By now the Ministry of Transport had announced it was to relinquish control of the company from 31 December 1947. During 1947 the company incurred a trading loss of over £30,000 which was borne by the Ministry for whilst a 25% increase on the pre-war carrying rates had been authorised by the ministry from 1 January 1947, working expenses were more than 120% the pre-war figure. The conditions also affected the railways and a further general rise in carrying rates of between 30% and 55% was authorised from 1 October 1947.

Despite this in the first six months of 1948 FMC incurred a trading loss of £5,000 and was faced with the prospect of a similar loss in the second half year. By now most of the railways and

The motor boat CRANE in a post Second World War livery. (Author's collection)

inland waterways had been nationalised to become part of the British Transport Commission. The waterways were administered by the Commission's Docks and Inland Waterways Executive, which had inherited a share holding in FMC from the Grand Union Canal Company giving it a close interest in the company's affairs.

The directors called an extraordinary meeting of the shareholders to be held in Birmingham on 30 September 1948 to discuss the situation and they suggested the shareholders might wish to consider the company being voluntarily wound up with the assets being realised.

The meeting decided on voluntary liquidation and a second extraordinary meeting in Birmingham was summoned for 2 November at which John Ironmonger and Edward Bosley were appointed as joint liquidators. FMC's board had met for the last time just prior to the meeting with all six directors attending.

The Docks and Inland Waterways Executive now stepped in and under an agreement dated 28 February 1949 the British Transport Commission agreed to purchase all of the company's craft and several of its premises.

107 motor boats and 65 butty boats with all their furniture & equipment	£42,000
Sherborne Street Wharf and warehouse, Birmingham (freehold)	47,250
Warwick Wharf, Fazeley Street, Birmingham (freehold)	32,000
Saltley Boat Dock (rented)	10,000
Leicester Wharf (surrender of lease)	375
Brentford Wharf (surrender of lease)	400
Uxbridge Wharf and Dock (surrender of lease)	nil
Broad Street Depot, Wolverhampton (surrender of lease held jointly with the London, Midland & Scottish Railway	nil
	£132,025

The properties were officially assigned to the British Transport

Members of Parliament together with directors from the canal company inspect YORK & GAILEY at Brentford in 1921 during a debate about a proposed Education Bill that would have led to restrictions on children living on narrow boats. (Canal Transport)

JAGUAR & FORWARD, still in FMC's colours, head northwards with a cargo of timber for Birmingham at Baker's Lane, near Knowle in July 1955. (Jack Parkinson)

Commission on 25 May 1949 and the boats on 30 July. At the same time the Commission also took over the equipment on the various wharves and in the warehouses, 18 motor lorries mostly based at Birmingham, 3 motor boat hulls in the course of construction at Yarwoods, 3 motor boat engines destined for these new hulls, and 4 boat horses making the total payment £149,197.

In July 1946 FMC had acquired the freehold of its leased premises in Wharf Road at the City Road Basin from the Grand Union Canal Company for £30,000. On liquidation this was now sold to Gibbons Skinner & Company who proceeded to fill in the side dock leading off the basin in order to extend their wharf by some 50ft across the dock entrance. The leased Nottingham wharf and warehouse passed to Nottingham City Council whilst the New Warwick Wharf was taken over by H. P. Sauce Limited, who had been important customers of FMC for many years. In

November 1949 the British Transport Commission purchased the freehold of Albion Wharf, Wolverhampton and probably at about the same time the Uxbridge wholesale coal business was sold to Charrington Booth Limited, which shortly afterwards became Charrington Warren Limited.

With these and other disposals the liquidators had been able to make a series of distributions to the shareholders of the 144,000 shares in issue and they amounted to £3. 9. 1¼d for each £1 share: -

Initial payment – 24 January 1949	20/- (£1) per share
Second payment – 7 April 1949	30/- (£1.50) per share
Third payment – 22 October 1949	12/6d (62½p) per share
Final payment – 30 November 1950	6/7¼d (33p) per share
Total	69/1¼d (£3.45½) per share

Meanwhile on 18 January 1950 at a meeting in Birmingham

Whilst FMC as a company ceased to exist soon after the Docks & Inland Waterways Executive took over most of its assets in 1949, many of its boats carried on under their new owners. Here the motors STAFFORD, still in its FMC livery, and SHAD, painted up in British Waterways' colours, are pictured at Runcorn Locks in the early 1950s. (Friths of Reigate)

the liquidators had presented a statement of accounts for their first 12 months to 2 November 1949, compensation of £6,500 was approved to be paid to the directors for loss of office and the liquidators remuneration of £4,512.10.0d was agreed. The final shareholders meeting was held at the Queen's Hotel in Birmingham on 5 December 1950 after the company's final two properties had been sold meaning the final distribution could be agreed and the liquidators could close their accounts.

Of the directors John Ironmonger retired from business having been with FMC for almost 60 years. He had been a leading authority on canal transport and had been awarded an OBE for his services to the Ministry of Food and the Ministry of Transport in the evacuation of tea and edible goods from the East London docks to inland buffer depots to protect them from enemy bombing in the Second World War. The company's boats had been heavily involved in this operation as many of the depots, such as the one at New Ground near Tring on the Grand Union Canal, were canal served. Ironmonger had also organised the safe custody of precious metals, such as tin and copper, and for arranging for local troops to load large quantities of copper to narrow boats in Birmingham with the steerers under orders to work fly to the docks to supply convoys destined for Russia.

For several years VIENNA, having been restored to its original 1911 condition, was moored at the Flint Mill Wharf, Cheddleton on the Caldon Canal. For most of her life with FMC she had carried the name VERBENA, but during the First World War several boats with names that could be linked to the enemy were renamed, hence AUSTRIA became AMESBURY, GERMANY became ENGLAND, RHINE became ROSE and VIENNA became VERBENA. (Author's collection)

Another long server, James Clayton, also retired but Ralph Ironmonger took over an ironmongery shop at Hall Green to become well-known in the area as "Ironmonger the ironmonger."

Most of the boatmen, the depot and warehouse staff and many of the clerks were taken on by the Docks & Inland Waterways Executive as were some of the managerial staff. The latter included Roger Holder at Wolverhampton, Sidney Ridding, chief clerk and cashier at Sherborne Street, Edmund Tart, cashier at Albion Wharf, George Claridge, supervisor at Fazeley Street, Leslie Painter, superintendent of the Southern Fleet, Wilfred Henman, manager of both Uxbridge and Saltley Dock and George Lively, manager of the Leicester and Nottingham depots. Several employees were taken on by H.P. Sauce Ltd. who had taken over the New Warwick Wharf.

With the acquisition of the FMC fleets the Docks & Inland Waterways Executive set about integrating the boats in with the Grand Union Canal Carrying Co. Ltd's fleet, which it had acquired with the nationalisation of the Grand Union Canal Company on 1 January 1948. Forty-five FMC pairs entered the South Eastern Division fleet, based at Bulls Bridge in Southall, but another 11 motors and 7 butties saw little further service and were either sold, scrapped or transferred to the maintenance fleet.

The Grand Union had not normally traded northwards from the West Midlands so FMC's fleet, based on Wolverhampton, formed a new trading area for the executive. Seventeen motors with 15hp Bolinders, 34 single motors with 9hp Bolinders, 9 butties paired with a motor and 5 unpaired butties formed the basis for a new North Western Division Southern Fleet, the

In 1982 PRESIDENT was sold to the Black Country Museum and West Midlands County Council. Then in 1984 a group of enthusiasts formed the Friends of President to support the maintenance and operation of the boat. As part of their very active involvement in 2009 they staged a re-enactment of the 1910 type trip through Long Buckby. (Richard Thomas)

Division's Northern Fleet consisting of the craft taken over from Canal Transport Limited based on the Leeds & Liverpool Canal.

At the time of the take-over three coppered-steel hulls were either in the course of construction at Yarwoods or in the course of fitting out at Saltley. The first, the single motor MALVERN, entered service on 12 September 1949 at a cost of £1645.10/- and she was followed a month later by MENDIP. The third hull, which was to become GORSE, was delivered firstly to Saltley where some fitting out work was done but was then moved to the Uxbridge yard and did not finally enter service until July 1951. This delay, though, was better than the fate of COTSWOLD, a new wooden motor boat that was being built at Uxbridge at the time of the take-over. Whilst construction was well advanced for reasons known only to

themselves, the D&IWE gave orders that the part-completed boat was to be scrapped. It was an ignominious end.

The purchase by the Docks & Inland Waterways Executive effectively saw the end of FMC as a major force in the canal carrying industry in this country. Its boats soon started losing their identity by being painted up in the British Waterways colours and many of them, especially the wooden ones, were either sold or scrapped.

Eventually the company's name reappeared when a plant hire company at Frodsham in Cheshire adopted it on 3 June 1981 and subsequently the name was sold to the Stourbridge Navigation Trust who registered a new FMC company on 13 November 1986.

CHILTERN, one of the last motor boats to be built for FMC, was still very much in active service as it locks down the Audlem flight on the Shropshire Union Canal on 17 June 1959. Whilst retaining its name it was allotted the fleet number 735/17 when all the boats in the North West fleet were renumbered in the middle of 1958. (Edward Paget-Tomlinson)

Hence the famous name lived on but at the same time many of the original boats have survived and several have been painted up in one or other of the two liveries to provide a reminder of an illustrious past.

(I would wish to express my gratitude to Richard Booth, Tom Foxon, Pete Harrison and Christopher M. Jones in particular and to many others too numerous to mention individually all of whom have given me their generous help during the preparation of this account. Whilst every effort has been made to be accurate, particularly over the fleet list, the absence of many of the early records means it is virtually inevitable some mistakes may have crept in and I would welcome hearing of any such errors.)

FELLOWS MORTON & CLAYTON LIMITED   FLEET LIST

Name	Joined fleet	Fleet No:	Registration	BCN Gauging	Fate
ACACIA (m)	YG 07.31	300	Bm 1535 – 24.07.31	1740 – 14.09.32	01.49 NWD
ACTON	RN 07.15	76	Bm 1338 – 16.07.15	18658 – 24.06.03	11.25 Erewash Canal Carrying Co
ADA	UG 07.22	1	Uxb 527	485 – 09.11.22	04.41 T. & S. Element Ltd
ADDER (m)	YA 04.23	285	Bm 1451 – 04.05.23	676 – 14.06.23	01.49 NWD
AFRICA	XF 01.89		Wv 636 – 18.09.88	12398 – 04.04.89	00.98 sold
AIRE	UR 05.17	50	Uxb 504 – 29.05.17	23211 – 22.07.20	01.49 SED
ALBERT	XS 08.21	176	Bm 1412 – 30.09.21	545 – 11.01.23	03.32 Grand Union Canal Company
ALBION	XF 01.89	16	Wv 676 – 04.06.89	17910 – 23.09.01	07.12 W. H. Green, Stoke on Trent
ALDER (m)	YG 09.31	301	Bm 1536 – 02.10.31	1787 – 11.12.33	01.49 NWD
ALEXANDER	XF 01.89		Bm 739 – 13.05.90	1396 – 20.05.90++	07.91 sold
ALEXANDRA	XP 04.90	89	Bm 779 – 17.07.91	19241 – 10.05.04	10.05 Adolphe Crosbie Ltd
ALICE (w)	XF 01.89		Lon 76 – 20.01.88	9431 – 14.09.94++	01.01 Thames Steam Tug
ALICE	UG 03.10	160	Uxb 447 – 23.03.10	Not gauged	01.31 scrapped
AMERICA	XF 01.89		Not 126 – 13.07.94	10730 – 15.06.88**	05.98 sold
AMESBURY	RN 11.14	106	Bm 1323 – 04.12.14	19933 – 02.01.06	01.49 SED
AMPLISS MARY	ZA 08.96		Bm 822 – 30.09.92	10856 – 06.08.96**	06.03 Henry Hirons
AMY	UG 09.22	3	Uxb 527 – 28.09.22	610 – 02.03.23	01.49 SED
ANGLESEY	SW 02.03	80	Bm 1108 – 06.06.03	18501 – 06.03.03	01.27 Midland Concrete Co, Ilkeston
ANKER	XW 06.89	140	Bm 863 – 30.06.93	16582 – 21.02.99	02.13 Smith Stone & Knight Ltd
ANKER	UR 06.17	51	Uxb 506 – 31.07.17	1308 – 15.07.27	11.39 Uxbridge coke boat
ANNIE	XP 06.97	221	Uxb 195 – 30.04.95	18508 – 09.03.03	04.14 Nottingham Coal Company
ANTELOPE (m)	YA 06.23	287	Bm 1452 – 05.07.23	978 – 11.12.24	01.49 SED
APOLLO (m)	XM 07.38	349	Bm 1626 – 19.02.43	1917 – 17.07.36	05.46 Ernest Thomas, Walsall
APPLE	UT 01.00	19	Uxb 286 – 27.03.00	21678 – 10.12.12	05.24 W. H. Green, Stoke on Trent
APPLE (m)	YG 01.32	302	Bm 1537 – 29.01.32	1878 – 20.11.35	01.49 NWD
APSLEY (w)	UV 11.96		Uxb 172 – 18.04.93	9279 – 17.12.96++	00.30 John Dickinson & Co. Ltd
ARABIA	SO 02.07	150	Bm 1188 – 05.04.07	20256 – 03.07.07	07.37 motor boat
ARABIA (m)	YU 07.37	150	Bm 1608 – 20.04.37	1975 – 18.08.37	01.49 NWD
ARIEL (m)	XM 07.38	351	Wv 1143 – 28.10.35	1871 – 26.08.35	01.49 NWD
ARRAS	XS 08.21	177	Bm 1421 – 21.10.21	630 – 31.03.23	09.30 Lees & Atkins, Polesworth
ARROW	XW 06.89		Bm 704 – 12.11.89	12713 – 10.04.90	11.07 Union Acid Co. Ltd
ARTHUR	XF 01.89		Bm 610 – 26.07.89	1396 – 20.05.90++	02.90 George Bull, Shukburgh
ARTHUR	XP 04.90		Bm 741 – 13.05.90	9313 – 14.09.94++	12.01 sold
ASIA	XF 01.89		Wv 616 – 17.04.88	1396 – 20.05.90++	00.04 sold
ASH	UT 01.00	15	Uxb 279 – 27.03.00	18573 – 28.04.03	01.23 scrapped
ASHTON	SW 05.95	181	Bm 937 – 25.05.95	17037 – 12.01.00	02.13 Smith Stone & Knight Ltd
ASTER	XD 07.98		Uxb 131 – 29.07.90	9622 – 03.09.94++	00.05 sold
ASTER (m)	UC 06.32	304	Uxb 579 – 28.06.32	12628 – 21.11.36**	01.49 SED
AUSTRALIA	SO 07.94	173	Bm 903 – 20.07.94	13894 – 24.10.94	01.49 SED
AUSTRIA	SO 06.05	106	Bm 1155 – 28.07.05	19933 – 02.01.06	11.14 renamed "Amesbury"
AVIS (m)	YA 06.23	286	Bm 1453 – 05.07.23	689 – 06.07.23	01.49 NWD
AVON	XF 01.89		Bm 802 – 19.02.92	9316 – 14.09.94++	10.94 Showells Brewery
AVON	ZB 09.02	51	Uxb 338 – 30.09.02	22469 – 20.03.16	02.17 Bratch Sand Company
AYLESBURY	UU 01.98	142	Uxb 233 – 28.06.98	17004 – 06.12.99	04.15 Union Acid Co. Ltd
AYLESTONE (w)	RE 09.97		Lcr 100 – 29.10.97	Not gauged	06.09 sold
AZALEA (m)	UC 09.32	305	Uxb 580 – 25.10.32	1769 – 19.07.33	01.49 SED
BADGER (m)	YA 06.23	288	Bm 1454 – 13.07.23	804 – 05.02.24	01.49 NWD
BALACLAVA	XF 01.89		Wv 194 – 25.03.79	1396 – 20.05.90++	00.91 sold
BANKER	XA 07.22	134	Bm 1446 – 18.11.22	1072 – 29.07.25	12.41 school boat
BARLASTON	XF 01.89		Bm 742 – 13.05.90	6910 – 21.03.74	10.00 sold
BARON (s)	SS 11.98	64	Bm 1015 – 23.12.98	11803 – 27.04.11**	02.15 motor boat
BARON (m)	SC 02.15	64	Bm 1015 – 23.12.98	22372 – 31.08.15	03.47 J. Holloway, Oldbury
BARONESS (s)	SS 11.98	240	Bm 1020 – 24.02.99	11698 – 19.04.11**	05.15 motor boat
BARTON	UU 10.99	186	Uxb 274 – 28.11.99	17041 – 16.01.00	08.16 Cadbury Brothers Ltd
BASCOTE	NB 05.29	89	Bm 1522 – 18.08.29	1651 – 22.12.30	01.49 SED
BEATRICE	UG 10.02	4	Uxb 528 – 31.10.22	627 – 27.03.23	06.48 Spencer Abbott & Co Ltd
BEAVER	XT 03.22	128	Bm 1434 – 17.03.22	116 – 04.10.21	06.43 scrapped
BEECH	UT 03.00	18	Uxb 287 – 27.03.00	18502 – 06.03.03	04.24 William Nurser & Sons
BEECH (m)	UD 03.35	328	Uxb 587 – 26.03.35	1942 – 27.01.37	01.49 SED
BEGONIA (m)	UD 01.35	309	Uxb 586 – 29.01.35	1920 – 07.08.36	01.49 SED
BELFAST	XF 01.89		Bm 796 – 24.12.91	9324 – 14.09.94++	03.95 Atlas Brick & Tile Co, Willesden
BELGIUM	SW 03.95	165	Bm 929 – 29.03.95	18189 – 29.05.02	05.20 Trent Navigation Company
BELGIUM	SO 08.05	107	Bm 1156 – 29.05.05	19936 – 04.01.06	07.42 Samuel Barlow Coal Co. Ltd
BELGRAVE	RD 09.96	187	Lcr 97 – 00.00.96	16585 – 22.02.99	05.13 Smith Stone & Knight Ltd
BERSHAM	XE 12.17	257	Uxb 509 – 28.05.18	20929 – 21.07.09	03.29 scrapped
BESSIE	UG 12.22	5	Uxb 529 – 28.12.22	549 – 17.01.23	01.42 Ernest Thomas, Walsall
BILSTON	XF 01.89	120	Bm 850 – 29.03.93	19529 – 22.11.04	04.15 Smith Stone & Knight Ltd
BIRCH	UT 03.00	30	Uxb 288 – 27.03.00	18777 – 13.10.03	09.22 scrapped at Uxbridge
BIRKENHEAD	XW 06.89	37	Bm 808 – 25.03.92	19574 – 04.01.05	04.07 J. Brough
BISON (m)	YA 12.23	289	Bm 1458 – 25.01.24	1302 – 22.06.27	01.49 SED
BLACKCOCK	XS 08.21	178	Bm 1413 – 30.09.21	1299 – 18.06.27	05.29 Nurser Brothers, Braunston
BLISWORTH (w)	XP 06.97		Uxb 71 – 22.02.87	10559 – 07.07.87**	08.05 Odell & Co., Paddington
BLUEBELL	XL 06.94	177	Bm 911 – 07.12.94	19329 – 02.07.04	05.12 Union Acid Co. Ltd
BOADICEA	XF 01.89		Bm 718 – 11.02.90	10620 – 05.07.83**	06.95 E. L. Hunt
BOMBAY	XF 01.89		Wv 413 – 09.10.82	1396 – 20.05.90++	00.95 sold
BOXMOOR	SW 03.95	178	Bm 933 – 26.04.95	15916 – 09.11.97	04.15 Smith Stone & Knight Ltd
BRAMBLE (m)	YK 07.34	307	Uxb 584 – 31.07.34	12458 – 06.03.36**	01.49 SED
BRAUNSTON	XP 06.97	222	Bm 234 – 28.06.98	17338 – 14.08.00	11.05 Worsey Ltd
BRAUNSTON (m)	UV 11.10	256	Uxb 453 – 29.11.10	11664 – 16.12.10**	12.15 War Department
BREAM (m)	YH 02.33	310	Bm 1545 – 24.02.33	1759 – 28.04.33	01.49 NWD
BRECON	SW 03.03	84	Bm 1110 – 11.05.03	18570 – 27.04.03	02.30 Lees & Atkins, Polesworth
BRENTFORD	XF 01.89		Wv 200 – 08.04.79	1396 – 20.05.90++	06.06 William Hunt & Sons Ltd
BRENTFORD	SW 12.02	74	Bm 1107 – 06.02.03	18568 – 25.04.03	05.28 Boots Pure Drug Co. Ltd
BRIAR (m)	UD 05.35	330	Uxb 588 – 23.05.35	12531 – 18.06.36**	01.49 SED
BRIGADIER	XS 08.21	181	Bm 1411 – 30.09.21	830 – 09.04.24	09.30 Lees & Atkins, Polesworth
BRILL (m)	UF 08.33	311	Uxb 582 – 05.08.33	1779 – 13.10.33	01.49 NWD
BRITON (m)	SC 05.15	240	Bm 1333 – 23.04.15	895 – 28.07.24	01.47 J. Dean & Sons
BUCKBY	UU 06.99	255	Uxb 267 – 25.07.99	17774 – 17.06.01	06.15 Cadbury Brothers Ltd
BUCKINGHAM	UU 06.98	12	Uxb 244 – 16.09.98	16707 – 11.05.99	11.25 H. McAndrews, Uxbridge
BUFFALO (m)	YA 01.24	290	Bm 1459 – 02.02.24	943 – 18.10.24	01.49 SED
BULBOURNE	ST 03.98	144	Bm 1004 – 06.05.98	16474 – 24.11.98	04.02 Ernest Thomas, Walsall
BURSLEM	ST 08.98	108	Bm 1012 – 05.10.98	16882 – 07.09.99	11.42 Imperial Chemical Industries
BURTON	SW 10.96	202	Bm 957 – 12.10.96	17509 – 05.11.00	12.16 Kynochs Ltd
BUTTERCUP	XD 07.98		Ilk 59 – 31.05.99	10078 – 10.08.74**	05.49 Alfred James Ash, Tipton
CACTUS (m)	YJ 05.35	329	Bm 1567 – 21.06.35	Not gauged	01.49 SED
CAERNARVON	UU 01.06	62	Uxb 400 – 30.01.06	19992 – 08.03.06	11.26 W. H. Green, Stoke on Trent
CAIRO (w)	XN 11.99		Lon 177 – 30.11.89	Not found	00.01 sold
CALCUTTA	XF 01.89	155	Wv 412 – 11.10.82	19237 – 10.05.04	01.07 J. B. Price, Burslem
CAMEL (m)	YA 04.24	291	Bm 1464 – 16.05.24	1013 – 12.02.05	01.49 SED
CAMELIA	XF 01.89		Wv 213 – 08.04.79	1396 – 20.05.90++	10.92 Benjamin Stevens, Sandiacre
CAPTAIN (m)	SC 07.24	217	Bm 1466 – 04.07.24	1000 – 23.01.25	05.47 Thomas Clayton (Oldbury) Ltd
CARDIGAN	UU 01.06	42	Uxb 401 – 30.01.06	19989 – 06.03.06	11.26 W. H. Green, Stoke on Trent
CARP (m)	UF 03.34	312	Uxb 583 – 10.03.34	1811 – 20.07.34	01.49 NWD
CEDAR	UT 04.00	14	Uxb 290 – 19.04.00	17347 – 16.08.00	08.24 F. & G. Moore, Albion
CEYLON	XF 01.89	136	Bm 905 – 28.09.94	15921 – 11.11.97	06.99 Messrs Hart
CHELFORD	RA 02.99	241	Bm 1025 – 10.03.99	16877 – 03.09.99	11.19 Gotham Company
CHESHIRE	UU 03.99	243	Uxb 262 – 30.05.99	18700 – 23.07.03	11.25 Dickinson & Henshall,

Shardlow

Name	Code	No.	Registration	Gauge	Date	Owner / Note
CHESTNUT	UT 04.00	26	Uxb 291 – 19.04.00	17686 – 20.04.01	09.26	Great Western Railway
CHESTER	XH 08.90	157	Bm 865 – 30.06.93	13577 – 24.07.93	07.02	William Foster
CHILTERN (m)	UH 09.46	352	Bm 1627 – 13.09.46	2263 – 06.11.46	01.49	NWD
CHINA	XF 01.89	107	Wv 661 – 26.03.89	12442 – 24.05.89	03.05	George Fletcher, Long Eaton
CHUB (m)	YH 03.34	313	Bm 1547 – 20.04.34	1806 – 18.06.34	01.49	NWD
CLARA	UG 04.23	7	Uxb 531 – 17.04.23	784 – 31.12.23	01.42	Ernest Thomas, Walsall
CLARENCE (w)	XX 03.92		Not 118 – 21.03.92	Not found	00.00	not known
CLEE (m)	UH 06.47	353	Uxb 599 – 25.06.47	Not gauged	01.49	NWD
CLEMATIS (m)	UH 12.47	354	Bm 1573 – 02.08.35	1882 – 06.01.36	01.49	NWD
CLENT	XE 12.17	258	Uxb 510 – 30.07.18	21236 – 10.02.11	05.29	Nurser Brothers, Braunston
CLENT (m)	UH 12.47	354	Uxb 600 – 28.01.48	Not gauged	01.49	NWD
CLEOPATRA	XS 08.21	175	Bm 1424 – 21.10.21	21337 – 21.07.11	09.30	Lees & Atkins, Polesworth
CLOVER (m)	YJ 09.35	332	Uxb 589 – 26.11.35	Not gauged	01.49	SED
CLYDE	XF 01.89	27	Bm 817 – 17.06.92	19577 – 05.01.05	02.07	J. B. Marriott
CLYDE	UR 10.18	52	Uxb 511 – 29.10.18	1372 – 01.02.28	02.41	T. Gough
COLE	XW 06.89	110	Bm 873 – 04.08.93	19515 – 11.11.04	12.11	Union Acid Co,. Ltd
COLONEL (s)	SS 06.99	65	Bm 1040 – 27.10.99	11697 – 11.04.11**	09.24	motor boat
COLONEL (m)	SC 09.24	65	Bm 1548 – 17.05.34	1307 – 14.07.27	11.41	Leonard Leigh Ltd
COLUMBIA	SO 05.07	151	Bm 1189 – 14.06.07	20608 – 23.05.08	01.39	motor boat
COLUMBIA (m)	YU 01.39	346	Bm 1623 – 03.02.39	2069 – 31.07.39	01.49	NWD
COLWICH	UU 01.08	157	Uxb 426 – 28.01.08	20689 – 09.09.08	01.30	scrapped
COMET	XF 01.89		Bm 772 – 22.05.91	8251 – 25.11.74	09.01	Adolphe Crosbie Ltd
CONSTANCE	UG 01.23	6	Uxb 530 – 30.01.23	792 – 15.01.24	07.42	Hooper
CONWAY	UR 04.19	59	Uxb 513 – 29.04.19	23194 – 25.06.20	02.42	J. Holloway, Oldbury
CORMORANT m	YA 04.24	292	Bm 1463 – 16.05.24	859 – 20.05.24	01.49	NWD
CORNWALL	LA 05.31	256	Tam 101 – 30.05.31	1707 – 04.01.32	01.47	Spencer Abbott & Co. Ltd
COSGROVE	XP 06.97	223	Uxb 153 – 31.03.91	16578 – 16.02.99	10.04	E. Pugh & Company
COTSWOLD	UH.00.00	355	Never completed	Not gauged	00.49	scrapped at Uxbridge
COUNT (s)	SS 06.99	47	Bm 1036 – 04.08.99	11675 – 26.01.11**	07.97	motor boat
COUNT (m)	SC 07.25	47	Bm 1036 – 04.08.99	1163 – 23.04.26	10.47	Ernest Thomas, Walsall
COUNTESS (s)	XF 01.89	217	Bm 719 – 25.02.90	9435 – 14.09.94++	06.97	rebuilt
COUNTESS (m)	SX 06.92	217	Bm 987 – 01.10.97	9435 – 14.09.94++	07.24	motor boat
COVENTRY	XF 01.89		Bm 836 – 27.01.93	9702 – 18.09.65**	10.97	sold
COWLEY	UU 03.98	231	Uxb 235 – 28.06.98	17033 – 11.01.00	11.15	Union Acid Co. Ltd
COWSLIP	XD 07.98		Uxb 136 – 31.09.90	9625 – 03.09.94++	00.05	sold
CRACOW	XS 08.21	182	Bm 1419 – 21.10.21	800 – 31.01.24	09.30	Lees & Atkins, Polesworth
CRANE (m)	YA 10.24	293	Bm 1470 – 17.10.24	979 – 11.12.24	01.49	SED
CREWE	UU 03.99	132	Uxb 263 – 30.05.99	17020 – 01.01.00	05.29	Nurser Brothers, Braunston
CRICK	XF 01.89	158	Bm 862 – 16.06.93	17697 – 02.05.01	08.05	Williams & Price
CROWN	XS 08.21	206	Bm 1423 – 21.10.21	21361 – 25.08.11	03.31	L. J. Speight & Co. Ltd
CROXLEY (w)	UV 11.96		Uxb 168 – 25.10.92	10882 – 05.11.96**	02.22	Canal Transport Ltd
CYPRESS (m)	YJ 10.35	333	Bm 1580 – 22.11.35	1886 – 27.01.36	01.49	NWD
DACE (m)	YH 05.34	314	Bm 1552 – 08.06.34	1810 – 13.07.34	01.49	NWD
DAFFODIL	XD 07.98	249	Bm 1028 – 14.04.99	19734 – 05.05.05	09.12	William Nurser & Sons
DAFFODIL (m)	UD 11.35	334	Uxb 590 – 26.11.35	12603 – 29.10.36**	01.49	SED
DAHLIA (m)	UD 02.36	335	Uxb 591 – 25.02.36	12641 – 30.11.36**	01.49	SED
DAISY	SG 01.91	141	Bm 773 – 22.05.91	13001 – 30.04.91	03.06	Union Acid Co. Ltd
DART	UR 07.19	245	Uxb 515 – 29.07.19	849 – 30.04.24	01.49	SED
DAUNTLESS	XI 02.97	219	Bm 989 – 01.10.97	18139 – 10.04.02	06.09	Walsall Lime & Fullers Earth Co
DAUNTLESS	XP 06.97		Not found	12001 – 01.10.97++	00.09	sold
DAVENTRY	XF 01.89		Bm 506 – 07.10.85	10609 – 30.01.83**	03.94	sold
DAVENTRY	SW 06.94	160	Bm 898 – 11.05.94	13819 – 20.06.94	06.09	Picton & Company
DAWLEY	ST 04.99	244	Bm 1027 – 14.04.99	17336 – 13.08.00	01.49	SED
DEE	XW 06.89	4	Bm 813 – 22.04.92	18606 – 20.05.03	12.14	Union Acid Co. Ltd
DEE	UR 10.19	247	Uxb 517 – 30.12.19	896 – 28.07.24	01.49	SED
DELVILLE	XS 08.21	207	Bm 1427 – 04.11.21	22675 – 26.05.17	09.30	Lees & Atkins, Polesworth
DENBIGH	SW 12.05	53	Bm 1164 – 12.01.06	19981 – 28.02.06	05.28	Boots Pure Drug Co Ltd
DENHAM	UU.06.98	116	Uxb 240 – 16.09.98	18200 – 03.06.02	01.15	Union Acid Co. Ltd
DENMARK	SO 09.05	10	Bm 1160 – 29.09.05	20379 – 09.10.07	01.49	SED
DERBY	SW 07.96	204	Bm 958 – 12.10.96	18146 – 18.04.02	06.23	scrapped
DERWENT	XF 01.89	131	Wv 535 – 23.03.86	11920 – 21.05.86	07.02	Adople Crosbie Ltd
DEVON	ZC 12.25	36	Bm 1483 – 22.01.26	1281 – 01.04.27	01.49	SED
DIAMOND	XM 07.38		Wv 1148 – 18.03.38	1417 – 21.08.28	06.44	Ernest Thomas, Walsall
DIGBY	SW 06.97	146	Bm 958 – 05.01.97	16352 – 01.09.98	06.24	Union Acid Co. Ltd
DILYS	UG 06.23	16	Uxb 532 – 26.06.23	785 – 31.12.23	01.49	NWD
DOLPHIN (m)	YA 09.24	294	Bm 1469 – 17.10.24	1032 – 23.03.25	01.49	NWD
DON	XG 12.89	43	Bm 771 – 14.01.90	17780 – 18.06.01	11.12	Brownhills Chemical Co.
DOROTHY	UG 07.23	22	Uxb 534 – 31.07.23	989 – 01.01.25	07.47	S. E. Barlow, Tamworth
DORSET	PE 03.26	49	Bm 1488 – 28.05.26	1262 – 05.03.27	01.49	SED
DORY (m)	YH 06.34	315	Bm 1553 – 20.07.34	1855 – 20.05.35	01.49	NWD
DOVE	XF 01.89	84	Bm 874 – 04.08.93	16837 – 12.08.99	10.01	Union Acid Co. Ltd
DOVE (m)	YA 01.25	295	Bm 1475 – 20.02.25	1068 – 22.07.25	01.49	NWD
DRAGON (m)	YA 01.25	296	Bm 1476 – 20.02.25	1071 – 28.07.25	01.49	NWD
DRAYTON	ST 05.99	252	Bm 1029 – 12.05.99	18622 – 27.05.03	01.49	SED
DREADNOUGHT (w)	ZD 11.96		Not 177 – 10.11.96	Not gauged	00.00	W. J. Cowlishaw, Shardlow
DREADNOUGHT (w)	XX 12.99	1	Not found	17354 – 20.08.00	00.08	sold
DUCHESS (s)	XF 01.89		Bm 678 – 12.03.89	1396 – 20.05.90++	05.93	H. & E. Humphrey, Abingdon
DUDLEY	SW 06.97	208	Bm 979 – 02.04.97	16380 – 14.09.98	01.16	J. Holloway, Oldburty
DUKE (s)	XF 01.89	162	Bm 677 – 12.03.89	1396 – 20.05.90++	03.95	rebuilt
DUKE (s)	SP 03.95	162	Bm 930 – 29.03.95	11810 – 16.06.11**	06.23	scrapped
DURBAN	SO 07.03	92	Bm 1113 – 15.10.03	19467 – 04.10.04	10.42	G. Mellor & Co. Ltd
DUTEOUS (s)	US 02.23	8	Bm 1448 – 02.03.23	Not gauged	08.24	motor boat
DUTEOUS (m)	SD 08.24	8	Bm 1448 – 02.03.23	1235 – 30.12.26	04.45	Ernest Thomas, Walsall
EAGLE (m)	YB 04.26	15	Bm 1485 – 24.05.26	1228 – 15.12.26	01.49	NWD
EALING	XB 03.99	152	Uxb 270 – 25.07.99	17339 – 14.08.00	02.10	H. Mills, Pennsett
EARL (s)	SU 06.95	180	Bm 939 – 28.06.95	11807 – 20.05.11**	11.25	Charles Court, Yiewsley
EBONY	UT 05.00	63	Uxb 295 – 26.06.00	22063 – 14.04.14	05.24	W. H. Green, Stoke on Trent
EDEN	XF 01.89		Wv 630 – 24.07.88	1396 – 20.05.90++	09.03	sold
EDITH	XP 06.97	224	Bm 1175 – 10.10.03	18373 – 17.11.02	12.11	Salt Union Ltd., Stoke Prior
EDITH	UG 02.26	23	Uxb 549 – 23.02.26	1177 – 15.07.26	07.40	W. E. Chivers & Sons Ltd
EGYPT (w)	XN 11.89		Lon 183 – 17.01.90	Not found	00.01	sold
EGYPT	SO 11.03	21	Bm 1119 – 01.01.04	19359 – 08.08.04	12.48	Ernest Thomas, Walsall
ELDER (m)	UD 05.36	336	Uxb 592 – 26.05.36	12533 – 19.06.36**	01.49	SED
ELIZABETH	XF 01.89		Bm 688 – 15.05.89	10756 – 18.03.90**	04.90	sold
ELIZABETH	XP 04.90		Bm 746 – 24.06.90	10512 – 04.05.83**	03.00	Robinson
ELIZABETH (w)	ZE 00.96		Not 120 – 21.03.92	Not gauged	00.00	not known
ELK	XG 12.89		Wv 665 – 26.03.89	9337 – 14.09.94++	00.99	Larkins
ELLESMERE	UU 01.07	148	Uxb 414 – 29.01.07	20301 – 20.08.07	02.30	Lees & Atkins, Polesworth
ELM	UT 05.00	58	Uxb 295 – 26.06.00	18600 – 18.05.03	03.24	S. Pritchard, Bewdley
ELSIE	UG 04.26	30	Uxb 550 – 27.04.26	1169 – 18.06.26	01.49	SED
EMILY	XP 04.90		Bm 773 – 13.05.90	10658 – 26.01.85**	00.92	sold
EMILY (w)	XP 06.97		Uxb 50 – 30.06.85	10568 – 22.06.88**	01.10	Gibbons & Co., Langley
EMMA	XF 01.89		Lcr 18 – 20.01.97	1396 – 20.05.90++	00.03	Trench Mining Co., Thrumpton
EMMA	XP 06.97	225	Uxb 137 – 28.11.90	16365 – 08.09.98	05.13	Nottingham Coal Company
EMPEROR (s)	SS 05.98	238	Bm 1006 – 03.06.98	11669 – 19.01.11**	04.17	motor boat
EMPEROR (m)	SC 04.17	238	Bm 1006 – 03.06.98	1079 – 27.08.25	04.48	Thomas Clayton (Oldbury) Ltd
EMPRESS (s)	XF 01.89	168	Bm 835 – 13.01.93	9437 – 14.09.04++	05.98	rebuilt
EMPRESS (s)	SX 05.98	168	Bm 1009 – 16.07.98	11687 – 27.02.11**	10.19	motor boat
EMSCOTE	WN 10.26	88	Bm 1494 – 19.11.26	1561 – 19.02.30	06.48	S. Clover
EMU (m)	YB 08.26	18	Bm 1490 – 02.07.26	1854 – 17.05.35	01.49	SED

ENA	UG 08.26	31	Uxb 552 – 31.08.26	12139 – 12.10.26**	01.49	SED
ENGLAND	XF 01.89	6		Wv 593 – 22.04.03	05.08	S. W. B. Stephen, Smethwick
ENGLAND	RN 08.14	99	Bm 1319 – 02.10.14	19563 – 21.12.04	02.38	motor boat
ENGLAND (m)	YU 02.38	340	Bm 1615 – 18.02.38	2011 – 18.03.38	01.49	NWD
ENVOY (m)	SC 10.19	168	Bm 1384 – 19.12.19	103 – 03.09.21	02.48	Ernest Thomas, Walsall
ERICA (m)	UD 02.37	337	Uxb 595 – 23.02.37	12768 – 05.04.38**	01.49	SED
ESSEX	LA 11.25	27	Tam 5 – 19.12.25	1175 – 12.07.26	11.38	Ellis, Uxbridge
ETRURIA	UU 09.99	184	Uxb 273 – 28.11.99	17087 – 27.02.00	09.20	S. C. Mitchell
EUROPE	XF 01.89		Not 125 – 13.07.94	1396 – 20.05.90++	05.95	scrapped
EUTOCA	XD 07.98	258	Bm 1030 – 12.05.99	18565 – 24.04.03	07.12	William Nurser & Sons
EVELYN	UG 03.27	60	Uxb 556 – 29.03.27	1362 – 07.12.27	07.46	Spencer Abbott & Co. Ltd
EVENLODE	UR 03.22	120	Uxb 523 – 28.03.22	525 – 14.12.22	01.49	SED
EXCELSIOR	XW 06.89		Bm 564 – 16.11.86	Not found	09.91	John Morris, West Bromwich
EXE	UR 06.21	110	Uxb 518 – 28.06.21	187 – 07.03.22	01.49	SED
EXHALL	XQ 02.99	245	Uxb 269 – 06.10.03	18771 – 06.10.03	01.15	Coventry Ordnance Works
EXPERIMENT	XF 01.89		Bm 708 – 10.12.89	9340 – 14.09.94++	09.99	Beardmore
FAIRYFIELD	XS 12.21	174	Bm 1435 – 31.03.22	581 – 06.02.23	11.41	J. Williams & Co., Birmingham
FALCON (m)	YB 09.26	19	Uxb 553 – 31.08.26	1215 – 22.10.26	01.49	SED
FANNY	ZF 06.96	193	Bm 953a – 26 .06.96	10881 – 30.10.96**	09.01	George Cutler, Bugbrooke
FANNY	UG 07.27	115	Uxb 559 – 26.07.27	1364 – 02.01.28	01.49	SED
FAY	UG 11.27	118	Uxb 560 – 29.11.27	1457 – 18.12.28	01.49	SED
FAZELEY	ST 08.21	113	Bm 1409 – 30.09.21	851 – 03.05.24	01.49	SED
FENNY	UU 01.98	36	Uxb 232 – 28.06.98	17002 – 06.12.99	08.12	W. Sharp, Derby
FERN (m)	YL 06.47	356	Bm 1629 – 11.07.47	Not gauged	01.49	SED
FERRET (m)	YB 10.26	58	Bm 1492 – 01.11.26	1231 – 21.12.26	01.49	NWD
FIDGET	XF 01.89		Bm 769 – 14.04.91	9342 – 14.09.94++	08.98	Richards
FINCHFIELD	XG 12.89		Wv 427 –07.08.83	Not found	09.95	sold
FIR	UT 07.00	72	Uxb 296 – 28.08.00	20254 – 02.07.07	02.24	William Nurser & Sons
FLINT	SW 01.06	87	Bm 1169 – 16.02.06	21240 – 15.02.11	09.26	Midland Concrete Co., Ilkeston
FLORENCE	UG 01.28	117	Uxb 561 – 31.01.28	1607 – 04.06.30	01.49	SED
FORGET ME NOT	XL 06.94	174	Bm 909 – 28.09.94	15746 – 30.07.97	07.12	W. H. Green, Stoke on Trent
FORWARD	XC 10.93		Bm 888 – 15.12.93	10852 – 29.07.96**	01.01	Salter & Company
FORWARD	ST 06.22	116	Bm 1440 – 30.06.22	1151 – 16.03.26	01.49	SED
FOX (m)	YC 11.26	63	Uxb 554 – 30.11.26	1586 – 14.04.30	01.49	SED
FOXGLOVE (m)	YL 12.47	357	Bm 1631 – 16.12.47	Not gauged	01.49	SED
FOXTON	ST 05.00	79	Bm 1058 – 27.07.00	18265 – 12.08.02	01.49	NWD
FRADLEY	UU 03.01	31	Uxb 316 – 26.02.01	Not gauged	11.19	Dunlop Ltd
FRANCE	SO 08.04	46	Bm 1140 – 30.09.04	19442 – 21.09.04	05.37	motor boat
FRANCE (m)	YU 05.37	338	Bm 1606 – 04.06.37	1963 – 11.06.37	01.49	NWD
FRANK	RD 07.15	97	Lcr 135 – 02.07.15	22440 – 25.01.16	03.32	Grand Union Canal Company
FREDA	UG 04.28	123	Uxb 562 – 29.05.28	1551 – 17.01.30	01.49	SED
FREDERICK	XF 01.89		Bm 590 – 19.04.87	9754 – 21.06.67**	07.91	Annie Sherwin, Loughborough
FREDERICK	XX 05.93		Bm 858 – 16.06.93	13531 – 15.05.93	12.01	J. E. Perry & Son
FUSCHIA	XD 07.98	55	Bm 1023 – 10.03.99	19342 – 12.07.04	01.11	Worsey Ltd
GAILEY	ST 10.99	35	Bm 1039 – 13.10.99	17146 – 03.04.00	08.37	motor boat
GAILEY (m)	YU 08.37	35	Bm 1609 – 20.08.37	2025 – 22.06.38	01.49	NWD
GAINSBORO	XF 01.89		Bm 702 – 22.10.89	9347 – 14.09.94++	08.98	W. E. Costin, Berkhamsted
GAMBIA	SO 06.07	154	Bm 1191 – 12.07.07	20367 – 28.09.07	08.38	motor boat
GAMBIA (m)	YU 08.38	344	Bm 1619 – 26.08.38	2045 – 07.10.38	01.49	NWD
GANGES	XF 01.89		Bm 706 – 12.11.89	11923 – 22.05.86	05.98	sold
GARDENIA (m)	YL 12.47	358	Bm 1632 – 16.12.47	Not gauged	01.49	SED
GAYTON	XP 06.97	226	Uxb 191 – 28.03.95	18352 – 04.11.02	02.14	Derby Canal Company
GENERAL (s)	SS 11.07	155	Bm 1192 – 29.11.07	11671 – 23.01.11**	05.24	motor boat
GENERAL (m)	SC 05.24	155	Bm 1192 – 29.11.07	1552 – 17.01.30	07.46	Ernest Thomas, Walsall
GEORGE	XG 12.89	130	Bm 812 – 22.04.92	13339 – 29.07.92	02.13	Union Acid Co. Ltd
GERANIUM	XD 07.98		Uxb 268 – 25.07.99	16644 – 06.04.99	00.05	sold
GERMANY	SO 11.04	99	Bm 1145 – 02.12.04	19563 – 21.12.04	08.14	renamed "England"
GERTIE	UG 07.28	137	Uxb 563 – 25.09.28	1790 – 08.01.34	01.49	SED
GLADYS	UG 12.28	146	Uxb 565 – 29.01.29	1647 – 18.11.30	01.49	SED
GLASGOW	ST 02.09	246	Bm 1211 – 05.03.09	21182 – 09.11.10	01.49	SED
GOOLE	BK 07.12	264	Bm 1264 – 09.07.12	21901 – 29.10.13	01.42	Ernest Thomas, Walsall
GORSE (m)	YL 03.51	359	Uxb 601 – 02.07.51	Not gauged	03.51	NWD
GOSPORT	BK 07.12	266	Bm 1266 – 01.08.12	21797 – 12.06.13	08.48	Ernest Thomas, Walsall
GRACE	UG 03.29	162	Uxb 566 – 26.03.29	1514 – 27.07.29	11.40	destroyed by enemy action
GRANGE	BK 05.12	261	Bm 1257 – 07.05.12	21799 – 12.06.13	01.49	SED
GRANTHAM	BK 06.12	262	Bm 1296 – 03.10.13	21982 – 02.02.14	04.45	Ernest Thomas, Walsall
GRAVESEND	XF 01.89		Bm 703 – 12.11.89	10629 – 24.09.83**	10.00	sold
GRAVESEND	BK 06.12	263	Bm 1261 – 05.07.12	21952 – 12.11.13	11.27	Boots Pure Drug Co. Ltd
GREAT BRIDGE	XF 01.89		Wv 25 – 08.04.79	4743 – 12.12.73	10.00	J. E. Perry & Son
GREET	BK 06.12	264	Bm 1262 – 09.07.12	21985 – 04.02.14	01.49	SED
GRETA	UG 08.29	180	Uxb 567 – 27.08.29	1679 – 22.06.31	01.49	SED
GREYHOUND (m)	YB 11.26	69	Bm 1493 – 29.10.26	1232 – 22.12.26	01.49	SED
GRIMSBY	ST 03.10	191	Bm 1217 – 11.03.10	21239 – 13.02.11	01.49	SED
GUILDFORD	XC 10.93		Bm 881 – 27.10.93	14892 – 09.03.96	05.99	Alfred James Ash, Tipton
HAMPTON	BK 08.12	267	Bm 1269 – 04.10.12	21941 – 05.12.13	03.45	Robert Teal Ltd, Newark
HANDSWORTH	XF 01.89		Bm 31 – 05.02.79	5339 – 31.12.73	02.00	Union Acid Co. Ltd
HANLEY	ST 01.99	253	Bm 1032 – 02.06.99	18540 – 01.04.03	07.38	motor boat
HANLEY (m)	YU 07.38	343	Bm 1618 – 15.07.38	2039 – 24.08.38	01.49	NWD
HANNAH	ZG.12.90		Bm 807 – 25.03.92	10786 – 12.12.90**	08.96	Edward Barrett, Sandiacre
HANWELL	ST 04.00	100	Bm 1057 – 13.07.00	18687 – 14.07.03	01.49	NWD
HAPPY RETURN	XG 12.89		Wv 487 – 04.08.85	1396 – 20.05.90++	00.90	sold
HARE (m)	YB 12.26	71	Bm 1495 – 03.12.26	1238 – 07.01.27	01.49	SED
HARECASTLE	ST 02.99	259	Bm 1035 – 07.07.99	17155 – 05.04.00	07.42	Oxford Canal Company
HAREFIELD (w)	UV 07.11	248	Uxb 459 – 25.07.11	11820 – 16.04.12**	12.15	War Department
HARTFORD	ST 12.98	215	Bm 1017 – 27.01.99	17190 – 01.05.00	01.49	SED
HATHERTON	XF 01.89		Wv 15 – 28.01.79	1396 – 20.05.90++	00.93	sold
HATTON	SW 03.96	188	Bm 949 – 27.03.96	18494 – 02.03.03	07.15	S. Allsopp & Sons Ltd., Burton
HAWK (m)	YC 03.27	70	Uxb 555 – 22.02.27	1846 – 13.03.35	01.49	SED
HAWKESBURY	XQ 02.99	245	Uxb 251 – 25.10.98	11083 – 28.07.99**	00.05	sold
HAYES	XB 03.99		Uxb 278 – 30.01.00	10721 – 30.09.87**	00.05	sold
HECLA (s)	XF 01.89	127	Bm 803 – 27.02.92	12330 – 15.01.89	11.21	rebuilt
HECLA (s)	US 04.22	127	Bm 1436 – 19.05.22	11914 – 22.09.22**	07.24	motor boat
HECLA (s)	SD 07.24	127	Bm 1436 – 19.05.22	1410 – 17.07.28	09.41	Samuel Barlow Coal Co. Ltd.
HELEN	UG 06.30	186	Uxb 574 – 24.06.30	12326 – 30.05.32**	01.49	SED
HEREFORD	BK 09.12	268	Bm 1271 – 04.10.12	22189 – 29.09.14	06.45	Manchester Ship Canal Co
HETTIE	XF 01.89		Wv 236 – 22.04.79	1396 – 20.05.90++	03.95	Atlas Brick & Tile Co, Willesden
HETTIE	SG 03.95	95	Bm 928 – 29.03.95	15871 – 14.10.97	05.23	scrapped
HETTIE	UG 03.30	185	Uxb 573 – 25.03.30	12325 – 03.05.22**	01.49	SED
HEYWOOD	XX 01.98	235	Bm 995 – 21.01.98	Not found	01.99	sold
HILDA	UG 12.29	158	Uxb 571 – 31.12.29	1692 – 04.09.31	01.49	NWD
HOCKLEY	SW 04.97	211	Bm 982 – 03.05.97	15840 – 23.09.97	01.17	Birmingham Metals & Munitions
HOLLAND	SO 12.05	40	Bm 1163 – 05.01.06	20278 – 27.07.07	06.37	motor boat
HOLLAND (m)	YU 06.30	40	Bm 1607 – 06.06.37	2008 – 25.02.38	07.09	motor boat
HONESTY	XD 07.98	256	Uxb 147 – 24.02.91	12985 – 15.04.91	07.04	Mary Ann Gilbert, Welford
HOPE	XF 01.89		Bm 735 – 13.05.90	10623 – 25.07.83**	10.00	sold
HUMBER	XW 06.89		Bm 705 – 12.11.89	8051 – 03.09.74	02.94	Isaac Slater, Alrewas
HYDE	SW 07.95	69	Bm 942 – 02.08.95	17341 – 15.08.00	01.17	Birmingham Metals & Munitions
IBEX (m)	YB 02.27	90	Bm 1497 – 05.02.27	1298 – 17.06.27	01.49	SED
IDA	UG 12.30	184	Uxb 575 – 30.12.30	1881 – 11.12.35	01.49	SED
ILFORD	BK 09.12	269	Bm 1272 – 04.10.12	21812 – 24.06.13	06.45	Manchester Ship Canal Co
ILKESTON	BK 09.12	270	Bm 1273 – 04.10.12	21961 – 23.12.13	06.45	Manchester Ship Canal Co

Munitions

Name	Reg.	No.	Build	Gauge	Date / Owner
IMOGEN	XS 12.21	143	Bm 1430 – 25.02.22	21352 – 16.08.11	03.31 Colonel Jardine
INDIA	SO 12.03	57	Bm 1123 – 12.02.04	19338 – 08.07.04	07.42 Oxford Canal Company
INDUSTRY	XP 06.97	220	Not found	12022 – 01.10.97++	04.00 Clark Brothers
IPSWICH	ST 04.12	222	Bm 1254 – 15.03.12	22008 – 23.02.14	01.49 NWD
IRELAND	XF 01.89	22	Bm 694 – 24.09.89	17662 – 28.03.01	09.12 William Nurser & Sons
IRENE	UG 04.31	192	Uxb 576 – 28.04.31	1761 – 10.05.33	01.49 NWD
IRIS	XD 07.98	66	Bm 1022 – 10.03.99	19651 – 01.03.05	08.13 A. W. Chilvers
ISIS	XW 06.89	100	Bm 869 – 14.07.93	16583 – 21.02.99	12.99 W. H. Simms
ISLEWORTH (w)	UV 01.12	89	Uxb 466 – 27.01.12	Not gauged	12.15 War Department
ISLINGTON (w)	UV 01.12	88	Uxb 465 – 30.01.12	Not gauged	12.15 War Department
ITALY	XF 01.89		Wv 443 – 13.10.84	11610 – 07.01.85	09.99 Thomas Jones, Wolverhampton
ITALY	SO 04.05	104	Bm 1149 – 07.04.05	19821 – 25.07.05	01.49 SED
IVER	XQ 02.99		Uxb 241 – 16.09.98	14007 – 27.04.00++	00.05 sold
IVER	ST 07.12	220	Bm 1260 – 05.07.12	21997 – 14.02.14	01.49 SED
IVINGHOE	XQ 02.99		Not found	11082 – 28.07.99**	00.05 sold
IVY	UT 07.00	78	Uxb 298 – 28.08.00	17397 – 10.09.00	04.26 Joseph Howard
IVY	UG 02.32	224	Uxb 578 – 23.02.32	1780 – 18.10.33	01.49 NWD
JACKAL (m)	YC 04.27	91	Uxb 557 – 29.03.27	12327 – 30.05.32**	01.49 SED
JAGUAR (m)	YC 05.27	95	Uxb 558 – 31.05.27	2166 – 11.08.43	01.49 SED
JAMES	XP 06.97		Uxb 188 – 31.07.94	Not found	00.00 not known
JAMES	BK 10.12	271	Bm 1274 – 08.11.12	22489 – 28.04.16	01.42 Ernest Thomas, Walsall
JANE	XP 04.90		Bm 732 – 22.04.90	10384 – 00.00.79**	06.00 W. Tolley
JAPAN	XT 12.03	11	Bm 1118 – 01.01.04	19573 – 03.01.05	01.42 Ernest Thomas, Walsall
JARROW	UU 04.12	152	Bm 659 – 30.04.12	21873 – 13.09.13	03.32 Grand Union Canal Company
JAVA	UO 04.12	153	Uxb 472 – 30.07.12	21908 – 04.11.13	03.32 Grand Union Canal Company
JERSEY	SO 04.10	141	Bm 1219 – 16.04.10	21249 – 01.03.11	01.49 NWD
JOAN	UG 02.33	231	Uxb 581 – 28.02.33	12769 – 05.04.38**	01.49 SED
JOHN	XP 04.90	210	Bm 736 – 13.05.90	10659 – 26.01.85**	04.01 Job Howard
JOHN	BK 12.12	272	Bm 1279 – 20.12.12	22029 – 09.03.14	01.49 NWD
JOSEPH	XP 04.90	88	Bm 738 – 13.05.90	12897 – 22.12.90	04.06 J. B. Price, Burslem
JUBILEE (m)	XM 07.38	347	Wv 1144 – 00.12.35	1873 – 06.09.35	12.41 Ernest Thomas, Walsall
JUNIPER	XD 07.98	257	Bm 1159 – 29.09.05	19209 – 26.04.04	09.07 J. B. Price, Burslem
JUPITER	XM 07.38		Wv 1087 – 02.08.22	556 – 22.01.23	12.38 River Severn Catchment Bd
KANGAROO (m)	YD 05.28	201	Bm 1509 – 18.06.28	1406 – 29.06.28	01.49 NWD
KATE	UG 05.10	164	Uxb 449 – 31.05.10	644 – 20.04.23	01.31 scrapped
KEGWORTH	ST 07.10	193	Bm 1223 – 15.07.10	21184 – 09.11.10	01.42 Ernest Thomas, Walsall
KERRY	RN 08.13	278	Bm 1295 – 22.08.13	21987 – 04.02.14	08.48 Ernest Thomas, Walsall
KESTREL (m)	YD 05.28	202	Bm 1510 – 28.06.28	1560 – 19.02.30	01.49 SED
KESWICK	ST 11.10	198	Bm 1228 – 16.12.10	22031 – 10.03.14	01.49 SED
KIDSGROVE	XX 01.98	230	Bm 1003 – 18.04.98	16793 – 07.07.99	12.99 Wilkinson & Company
KIDSGROVE	BK 02.13	273	Bm 1281 – 31.01.13	21986 – 04.02.14	11.42 Samuel Barlow Coal Co Ltd
KILBURN	ST 05.10	121	Bm 1220 – 17.06.10	21192 – 02.12.10	07.48 Ernest Thomas, Walsall
KILDARE	BK 03.13	274	Bm 1287 – 14.03.13	21743 – 10.04.13	08.48 Ernest Thomas, Walsall
KILSBY	BK 04.13	275	Bm 1288 – 02.05.13	129 – 20.10.21	06.45 Manchester Ship Canal Co
KIMBERLEY	SO 03.03	83	Bm 1111 – 22.05.03	18724 – 15.08.03	05.38 motor boat
KIMBERLEY (m)	YU 05.38	341	Bm 1616 – 27.05.38	2020 – 27.05.38	01.49 NWD
KINETON	BK 05.13	276	Bm 1289 – 23.05.13	22071 – 24.04.14	04.43 Samuel Barlow Coal Co Ltd
KING (m)	SC 06.25	103	Bm 1549 – 17.05.34	1236 – 31.12.36	07.47 Ernest Thomas, Walsall
KINGCUP	XD 07.98	167	Bm 1024 – 10.03.99	17632 – 05.03.01	09.07 J. B. Price, Burslem
KINGSBURY	BK 06.13	277	Bm 1294 – 20.06.13	22659 – 03.05.17	04.45 Ernest Thomas, Walsall
KINGSTOWN	BK 08.13	278	Bm 1295 – 22.08.13	21987 – 04.02.14	08.13 renamed "Kerry"
KINGSWOOD	SW 02.01	136	Bm 1068 – 22.02.01	18625 – 28.05.03	01.27 W. H. King, Glascote
KNOWLE	SW 06.96	201	Bm 954 – 26.06.96	15917 – 09.11.97	12.16 Kynochs Ltd
LAMPREY (m)	YI 08.34	316	Bm 1555 – 07.09.34	1885 – 24.01.36	01.49 NWD
LANCASTER	UU 01.07	149	Uxb 415 – 29.01.07	20355 – 19.09.07	02.30 Lees & Atkins, Polesworth
LANGLEY	UU 05.98	232	Uxb 236 – 28.06.98	16588 – 23.02.99	01.17 Birmingham Metals &
LAPWING (m)	SM 08.13	43	Bm 1299 – 03.10.13	21874 – 15.09.13	01.49 NWD
LARCH	UT 07.00	90	Uxb 297 – 28.00.00	18488 – 25.02.03	02.24 William Nurser & Sons
LARK	XW 06.89	106	Bm 849 – 09.03.93	12358 – 19.02.89	06.03 S. Dyehouse
LARK (m)	SM 10.13	44	Bm 1301 – 31.10.13	22270 – 01.02.15	01.49 SED
LAUREL (m)	SM 12.13	45	Bm 1304 – 19.12.13	21980 – 02.02.14	01.49 SED
LAURETTA	XF 01.89	135	Bm 759 – 09.12.90	11195 – 30.05.83	10.02 S. Dyehouse
LEA	XW 06.89	97	Not found	19370 – 16.08.04	01.06 sold
LEAM	XF 01.89		Bm 684 – 09.04.89	1396 – 20.05.90++	03.90 sold
LEAMINGTON	SW 04.96	190	Bm 952 – 04.05.96	15911 – 08.11.97	03.16 S. S. Sharp
LEICESTER	XF 01.89		Bm 785 – 31.07.91	11074 – 21.07.99**	10.00 Union Acid Co. Ltd
LEICESTER	ZH 12.25	41	Bm 1484 – 22.01.26	1167 – 19.05.26	03.41 Imperial Chemical Industries
LEIGHTON	ST 01.98	13	Bm 998 – 25.02.98	16059 – 14.02.98	04.41 Ernest Thomas, Walsall
LEMON	UT 09.00	101	Uxb 303 – 29.01.01	17682 – 19.04.01	02.28 Nurser Brothers, Braunston
LEO	XG 12.89	50	Bm 716 – 11.02.90	12575 – 12.11.89	01.14 Union Acid Co. Ltd
LEOPARD (m)	SM 12.12	37	Bm 1275 – 08.11.12	22017 – 27.02.14	01.49 SED
LIBERTY	XG 12.89	38	Bm 819 – 19.08.92	16764 – 22.06.99	04.07 Worsey Ltd
LICHFIELD	XH 08.90		Bm 778 – 19.06.91	9364 – 14.09.94++	01.00 Salter & Company
LIFFEY	XP 04.90	111	Bm 773 – 13.05.90	12833 – 15.09.90	11.04 Isaac Slater, Alrewas
LILAC	XD 07.98	59	Uxb 156 – 30.06.91	18680 – 10.07.03	11.15 Cadbury Brothers Ltd
LILY	XP 04.90		Bm 740 – 13.05.90	10703 – 30.04.87**	06.01 William Russell, Marsworth
LILY	XB 03.99		Not found	12010 – 16.05.99++	00.00 not known
LILY (m)	SM 02.14	55	Bm 1308 – 30.01.14	22233 – 19.11.14	01.49 SED
LINDA	SM 04.12	260	Bm 1290 – 30.01.14	21911 – 06.11.13	01.49 SED
LINDOLA	UA 08.12	33	Uxb 474 – 27.08.12	21734 – 27.03.13	05.37 Thomas Clayton (Oldbury) Ltd
LINFORD	XP 06.97	227	Lon 372 – 06.11.00	18595 – 14.05.03	11.12 Clay & Company, Brierley Hill
LING (m)	YI 10.34	317	Bm 1556 – 16.11.34	1834 – 30.11.34	01.49 NWD
LINSLADE	XP 06.97	234	Lon 371 – 06.11.00	18489 – 26.02.03	05.13 Nottingham Coal Company
LION (m)	SM 03.13	38	Bm 1286 – 19.03.13	21801 – 13.06.13	01.49 SED
LIVERPOOL	XF 01.89	113	Bm 691 – 25.07.89	18612 – 25.05.03	05.10 Worsey Ltd
LIVERPOOL	XW 06.89		Bm 550 – 28.09.86	11734 – 12.06.85	12.89 sold
LONGFORD	XQ 02.99	248	Uxb 248 – 25.10.98	18493 – 27.02.03	04.07 Worsey Ltd
LONGTON	ST 10.98	32	Bm 1014 – 28.10.98	16492 – 07.12.98	04.45 Ernest Thomas, Walsall
LOTUS (m)	SM 03.14	66	Bm 1310 – 20.03.14	22266 – 30.01.15	01.49 SED
LOUISA (w)	XF 01.89		Lon 290 – 27.10.96	9433 – 14.09.94++	05.99 Tough & Henderson
LUDLOW	XF 01.89	109	Bm 838 – 27.01.93	12467 – 27.06.89	05.12 William Nurser & Sons
LUPIN (m)	SM 03.14	67	Bm 1314 – 01.05.14	22286 – 16.03.15	01.49 SED
LURLINE (w)	XN 11.89		Lon 184 – 31.01.90	1396 – 20.05.90++	08.94 Tough & Henderson
LYNX (m)	SM 06.13	39	Bm 1290 – 30.05.13	21851 – 19.08.13	01.49 SED
MADELEY	HA 02.38	165	Bm 1502 – 31.03.28	1421 – 30.08.28	01.49 NWD
MADRAS	XF 01.89		Wv 387 – 19.07.81	1396 – 20.05.90++	00.03 sold
MAJESTIC (ow)	XU 01.12		Not registered	Not gauged	02.15 scrapped at Uxbridge
MALVERN	HA 07.28	166	Bm 1512 – 05.10.28	1423 – 13.09.28	11.42 Samuel Barlow Coal Co Ltd
MALVERN	YM 09.49	360	Bm 1634 – 16.09.49	Not gauged	09.49 NWD
MANCHESTER	XF 01.89		Bm 848 – 08.06.80	9369 – 14.09.94++	00.09 Phipkin & Palmer, Yiewsley
MAPLE	UT 09.00	115	Uxb 304 – 29.01.01	18513 – 11.03.03	03.26 Erewash Canal Company
MARGARET	XP 04.90		Bm 748 – 24.06.90	9368 – 14.09.94++	04.01 sold
MARGARET	XM 07.38	350	Tam 103 – 11.11.38	1796 – 21.02.34	04.41 John Whalley, Stoke on Trent
MARIA	XF 01.89	99	Bm 776 – 29.05.91	15461 – 20.01.97	12.01 J. Wainwright
MARPLE	SW 06.95	41	Bm 943 – 02.08.95	17340 – 14.08.00	08.16 Cadbury Brothers Ltd
MARQUIS (s)	SS 03.98	237	Bm 1002 – 18.03.98	16089 – 05.03.98	03.25 motor boat
MARQUIS (m)	SC 03.25	237	Bm 1533 – 16.01.31	1547 – 02.01.30	02.42 J. Holloway, Oldbury
MARSWORTH	UU 05.98	233	Uxb 234 – 16.09.98	16589 – 23.02.99	04.16 H. J. Chapman
MAUD	SG 03.97	207	Bm 974 – 05.03.97	14084 – 27.04.00++	08.13 Cafferata & Company, Newark
MAY	SG 03.97	206	Bm 973 – 05.03.97	21223 – 17.10.11	08.13 Cafferata & Company, Newark
MAYFLOWER (w)	XX 03.92		Not 119 – 21.03.92	Not gauged	00.00 not known
MAYFLOWER	XD 07.98		Not 132 – 07.06.99	18662 – 29.06.03	10.04 L. B. Faulkner, Leighton

Name	Reg	No	Builder – Date	Gauge No – Date	Buzzard	Owner / Notes
MEDWAY	XW 06.89		Bm 692 – 25.07.89	12408 – 11.04.89	02.01	J. E. Perry & Son
MENDIP (m)	YM 10.49	361	Bm 1635 – 11.11.49	Not gauged	10.49	NWD
MERCURY	XM 07.38		Wv 1120 – 13.06.26	1173 – 01.07.26	08.45	Samuel Barlow Coal Co Ltd
MERIONETH	WE 01.06	96	Ber 425 – 10.02.06	13984 – 25.07.06	05.27	Erewash Canal Company
MERMAID	XM 07.38		Wv 1118 – 26.10.25	774 – 12.12.23	12.38	River Severn Catchment Bd
MERSEY	XW 06.89	3	Bm 771 – 22.05.91	10909 – 21.02.82	09.07	J. B. Price, Burslem
MIDDLESEX	UU 01.03	76	Uxb 344 – 24.02.03	18658 – 24.06.03	07.15	renamed "Acton"
MIDDLESEX	LA 04.30	255	Tam 89 – 05.04.30	1612 – 17.06.30	08.48	Ernest Thomas, Walsall
MINNOW (m)	YI 12.34	318	Bm 1557 – 28.12.34	1896 – 01.04.36	01.49	NWD
MONARCH (s)	SS 04.08	156	Bm 1201 – 22.05.08	11813 – 04.07.11**	01.25	motor boat
MONARCH (m)	SC 01.25	156	Bm 1201 – 22.05.08	1412 – 19.07.28	10.46	F. J. Gopsill, Walsall
MONMOUTH	UU 05.06	135	Uxb 409 – 22.08.06	20117 – 06.12.06	07.27	Nurser Brothers, Braunston
MONTGOMERY	WE 01.06	124	Ber 426 – 10.02.06	13994 – 15.08.06	05.27	Erewash Canal Company
MOORE	RA 04.99	250	Bm 1031 – 02.06.99	16971 – 17.11.99	02.18	Union Acid Co. Ltd
MULLET (m)	YI 12.34	319	Bm 1558 –18.01.35	1847 – 22.03.35	01.49	NWD
MUNITION	XS 08.21	213	Bm 1425 – 21.10.21	22644 – 05.04.17	03.32	Grand Union Canal Company
MURIEL	XF 01.89	74	Bm 1000 – 18.03.98	16820 – 24.07.99	12.02	Charles Lane, Ansty
MYRTLE	XD 07.98	214	Uxb 272 – 28.11.99	14313 – 01.06.95	11.07	Derby Cooperative Society
NANCY	SG 02.94		Bm 896 –10.02.94	9371 – 14.09.94++	12.01	Robinson
NANTWICH	XE 12.17	256	Uxb 508 – 18.05.18	20180 – 15.03.07	07.42	Erewash Canal Company
NAPTON	UU 06.99	254	Uxb 266 – 25.07.99	16756 – 20.06.99	11.26	scrapped
NATAL	SO 10.03	93	Bm 1117 – 27.11.03	19471 – 07.10.04	01.49	SED
NAUTILUS	XX 11.99		War 125 – 12.12.99	14107 – 27.04.00++	01.49	SED
NAUTILUS (m)	YD 06.28	204	Bm 1511 – 28.06.28	1545 – 02.01.30	01.49	SED
NELSON	XF 01.89		Bm 710 – 14.01.90	11835 – 21.12.85	01.02	sold
NENE	XW 06.89	34	Bm 851 – 29.03.93	17035 – 12.01.00	08.13	James Parker
NEPTUNE	XM 07.38		ByH 293 – 05.02.23	1091 – 11.09.25	08.45	River Severn Catchment Bd.
NETHERTON	SW 01.97	166	Bm 970 – 29.03.97	16085 – 03.03.98	09.16	A. J. Harmsworth, Aldershot
NETTLE	XD 07.98		Pad 181 – 03.03.96	Not found	00.05	sold
NILE	XW 06.89		Bm 866 – 14.07.93	1396 – 20.05.90++	06.95	William Hunt & Sons
NORFOLK	LA 07.30	243	Tam 92 – 26.07.30	1632 – 18.09.30	09.48	sold
NORTHOLT	ST 12.98	75	Bm 1042 – 08.12.99	17712 – 11.05.01	07.42	Samuel Barlow Coal Co. Ltd
NORTHWICH	ST 12.98	242	Bm 1021 – 24.02.99	17139 – 29.03.00	01.49	NWD
NORTON	XP 06.97	228	Uxb 230 – 29.03.98	18374 – 17.11.02	02.13	William Nurser & Sons
NORWAY	SO 01.06	111	Bm 1165 – 12.01.06	20058 – 24.08.06	05.28	Boots Pure Drug Co. Ltd
NORWOOD	ZI 09.02	1	Bm 1099 – 10.10.02	18376 – 17.11.02	05.15	William Nurser & Sons
OAK	UT 10.00	119	Uxb 306 – 29.01.01	17781 – 18.06.01	11.25	Dickinson & Henshall, Shardlow
OHIO	XW 06.89	8	Bm 852 – 29.03.93	12109 – 15.10.87	06.05	scrapped
OLDBURY	ST 02.00	48	Bm 1046 – 16.02.00	17051 – 25.01.00	07.42	L. M.S. Railway Company
OLIVE	XD 07.98		Uxb 254 – 31.01.99	17005 – 07.12.99	06.20	Trent Navigation Company
OLTON	UU 01.00	192	Uxb 280 – 27.03.00	17091 – 28.02.00	03.26	William Nurser & Sons
OPHELIA	XS 08.21	219	Bm 1428 – 04.11.21	1143 – 27.02.26	03.32	Grand Union Canal Company
ORANGE	UT 11.00	118	Uxb 308 – 29.01.01	18683 – 11.07.03	03.24	W. H. Green, Stoke on Trent
ORION	XM 07.38		Wv 1127 – 14.01.29	832 – 09.04.24	04.41	T. & S. Element Ltd
ORWELL (w)	XX 07.89		Not found	10578 – 05.07.89**	07.09	sold
ORWELL	XX 06.99		Bm 1055 – 22.06.00	11063 – 08.07.99**	08.03	J. E. Perry & Son
OSTRICH (m)	YD 08.28	209	Bm 1514 – 05.10.28	1455 – 13.12.28	01.49	SED
OTHELLO	XS 08.21	221	Bm 1429 – 16.12.21	22186 – 25.09.14	03.32	Grand Union Canal Company
OTTER	ZJ 04.96	191	Bm 952a – 04.05.96	9309 – 16.04.96++	12.07	sold
OTTER (m)	YD 12.28	210	Bm 1517 – 27.03.29	1474 – 28.03.29	01.49	NWD
OUSE	XP 04.90		Bm 727 – 22.04.90	10707 – 09.05.87**	10.00	sold
OUSE (ow)	XU 01.12		Not registered	Not gauged	02.15	scrapped at Uxbridge
OWL (m)	YD 12.28	211	Bm 1516 – 15.02.29	1919 – 07.08.36	01.49	SED
OXFORD	XF 01.89		Bm 714 – 28.01.90	10858 – 08.08.96**	07.01	Tough & Company
PANSY	XD 07.98	2	Not 133 – 13.11.99	18251 – 21.07.02	09.04	L.B. Faulkner, Leighton
PANTHER (m)	YE 02.30	250	Bm 1526 – 21.02.30	1600 – 15.05.30	01.49	SED
PEACOCK (m)	SN 12.15	102	Bm 1342 – 30.11.15	22821 – 28.03.18	01.49	SED
PEAR	UT 12.00	73	Uxb 311 – 26.02.01	17595 – 30.01.01	09.30	Lees & Atkins, Polesworth
PEARL (w)	XN 11.89		Lon 176 – 06.11.89	1396 – 20.05.90++	08.94	Tough & Henderson
PEMBROKE	UU 03.06	126	Uxb 405 – 22.02.06	13980 – 25.07.06	03.29	Uxbridge coke boat
PENDLETON	XF 01.89		Wv 356 – 08.06.80	4705 – 12.12.73	00.98	Cupitt
PENGUIN (m)	SN 06.14	77	Bm 1316 – 17.07.14	22190 – 29.09.14	01.49	SED
PENKRIDGE	ST 01.98	56	Bm 999 – 25.02.98	16088 – 05.03.98	01.49	SED
PERCH (m)	YI 03.35	320	Bm 1560 – 15.03.35	1848 – 01.05.35	01.49	NWD
PERSEVERANCE	XF 01.89	10	Lcr 16 – 00.00.97	12108 – 30.09.87	05.05	A. Frost
PERSIA	SO 03.08	133	Bm 1198 – 13.03.08	20623 – 23.06.08	01.49	NWD
PETREL (m)	SN 10.14	81	Bm 1320 – 16.10.14	22289 – 26.03.15	01.49	SED
PHOEBE (w)	XP 06.97		Uxb 102 – 24.04.88	10577 – 04.07.89**	00.07	Thomas Turner, Yiewsley
PHOENIX (s)	XF 01.89	54	Bm 440 – 16.07.84	1396 – 20.05.90++	12.93	rebuilt
PHOENIX	SV 12.93	54	Bm 886 – 01.12.93	13795 – 12.05.94	09.25	scrapped
PIKE (m)	YI 04.35	321	Bm 1561 – 17.05.35	1856 – 29.05.35	01.49	NWD
PILOT (m)	SC 12.24	169	Bm 1329 – 20.02.25	12787 – 14.09.38**	07.41	Ernest Thomas, Walsall
PINE	UT 11.00	125	Uxb 309 – 29.01.01	17689 – 25.04.01	09.30	Lees & Atkins, Polesworth
PIONEER	XG 12.89	45	Bm 713 – 14.01.90	19516 – 11.11.04	07.12	William Nurser & Sons
PIONEER	XA 07.22	130	Bm 1443 – 29.09.22	814 – 17.03.24	07.42	Lees & Atkins, Polesworth
PIONEER (wm)	UW 10.34	308	Uxb 585 – 30.10.34	12400 – 14.10.35**	02.36	Harefield Lime Co. Ltd
PIRATE (s)	XW 06.89	124	Bm 859 – 16.06.93	1396 – 20.05.90++	06.94	rebuilt
PIRATE (s)	SV 06.94	124	Bm 900 – 16.06.94	9440 – 14.09.94++	12.02	Thomas Conservancy
PLOVER	XV 10.91	102	Bm 792 – 13.11.91	11503 – 20.07.84	03.08	scrapped
PLOVER (m)	SN 01.15	94	Bm 1325 – 18.12.14	22305 – 19.04.15	01.49	SED
PLYMOUTH	XF 01.89		Wv 296 – 15.07.79	9173 – 09.06.80**	00.02	J. E. Perry & Son
POLE STAR (m)	XF 01.89		Wv 1142 – 12.03.34	1792 – 10.01.34	08.39	Ernest Thomas, Walsall
POLLY	WE 06.99	8	Ber 283 – 07.06.99	17657 – 25.03.01	11.14	D. Marlow
POPLAR	UT 01.01	85	Uxb 314 – 26.02.01	18491 – 27.02.03	08.27	Nurser Brothers, Braunston
PORTUGAL	SO 06.06	145	Bm 1180 – 27.07.06	20191 – 11.04.07	10.37	motor boat
PORTUGAL	YU 10.37	339	Bm 1610 – 25.10.37	2003 – 14.01.38	01.49	NWD
PRESIDENT (s)	SS 06.09	195	Bm 1212 – 23.06.09	11682 – 20.02.11**	05.25	motor boat
PRESIDENT (m)	SC 05.25	195	Bm 1541 – 15.04.32	1832 – 21.11.34	06.46	Ernest Thomas, Walsall
PRESTON	XF 01.89		Wv 602 – 29.11.87	9383 – 14.09.94++	00.08	Trife
PRESTON	UU 09.08	163	Uxb 432 – 29.09.08	20801 – 12.01.09	02.29	Grand Union Canal Company
PRETORIA	SO 01.03	82	Bm 1109 – 06.03.03	18660 – 26.06.03	01.49	SED
PRIMROSE	XI 02.97	143	Bm 984 – 04.06.97	18655 – 24.06.03	01.14	Union Acid Co. Ltd
PRINCE (s)	SS 10.98	20	Bm 1011 – 05.10.98	11672 – 24.01.11**	03.26	motor boat
PRINCE (m)	SC 03.26	20	Bm 1534 – 20.02.31	12145 – 19.10.26**	11.41	Oxford Cooperative Society
PRINCESS (s)	XF 01.89	169	Wv 616 – 03.04.88	1396 – 20.05.90++	06.96	rebuilt
PRINCESS	XG 12.89		Wv 470 – 13.04.85	1396 – 20.05.90++	00.92	sold
PRINCESS (s)	SX 06.96	169	Bm 959 – 12.10.96	9439 – 14.09.94++	12.24	motor boat
PROSPEROUS	XF 01.89		Wv 229 – 22.04.79	9384 – 14.09.94++	00.02	J. E. Perry & Son
PROVIDENCE	XX 09.98		Uxb 239 – 16.09.98	Not found	00.00	not known
PYTHON	YF 02.30	249	Bm 952 – 25.02.30	Not gauged	01.49	SED
QUAIL (m)	UA 07.16	109	Bm 1348 – 28.07.16	22583 – 27.10.16	01.41	rebuilt
QUAIL (m)	UX 01.41	109	Uxb 598 – 25.01.41	22583 – 27.10.16	01.49	SED
QUEBEC	SO 09.10	197	Bm 1225 – 30.09.10	22075 – 29.04.14	11.42	Imperial Chemical Industries Ltd
QUEEN (s)	XF 01.89	9	Wv 591 – 20.06.87	12326 – 10.01.89	11.16	converted to open boat
RADFORD	RD 04.12	86	Lcr 130 – 12.04.12	22001 – 17.02.14	03.32	Grand Union Canal Company
RADNOR	UU 03.06	129	Uxb 404 – 22.02.06	13979 – 25.07.06	02.30	Lees & Atkins, Polesworth
RAMBLER (m)	UA 08.18	187	Bm 1369 – 13.09.18	23212 – 22.07.20	07.41	rebuilt
RAMBLER	UX 07.41	187	Uxb 597 – 13.09.18	23212 – 22.07.20	01.49	SED
RAVEN (m)	UA 07.17	200	Bm 1360 – 13.07.17	22793 – 06.12.17	05.40	rebuilt
RAVEN (m)	UX 05.40	200	Uxb 597 – 00.06.40	22793 – 06.12.17	01.49	SED

Name	Reg	No	Register	Gauge	Date	Owner / Note
REX	XG 12.89		Bm 877 – 29.09.93	9389 – 14.09.94++	04.02	Adolphe Crosbie Ltd
RHINE	XW 06.89	19	Bm 699 – 22.10.89	16518 – 30.12.98	01.00	Slater & Company
RHINE	BK 11.13	280	Bm 1302 – 31.10.13	22269 – 02.02.15	07.17	renamed "Rose"
RIBBLE	XW 06.89	42	Not found	19371 – 16.08.04	01.06	sold
RICHMOND	XC 10.93		Bm 887 – 01.12.93	9388 – 14.09.94++	05.98	Roper
ROACH	XI 02.97	205	Bm 971 – 05.02.97	9273 – 15.01.97++	04.01	sold
ROACH (m)	YI 12.35	322	Bm 1581 – 21.02.36	1911 – 24.06.36	01.49	NWD
ROBIN (m)	UA 04.19	188	Uxb 514 – 29.04.19	23328 – 10.01.21	11.40	destroyed by enemy bombing
ROCHDALE	UU 02.08	158	Uxb 427 – 28.01.08	22831 – 24.04.18	05.29	Nurser Brothers, Braunston
ROE	XG 12.89	24	Bm 945 – 11.10.95	16344 – 27.08.98	12.10	G. Heeley
ROMFORD	BK 12.13	281	Bm 1303 – 19.12.13	22060 – 08.04.14	01.49	SED
ROSE	XP 06.97	229	Uxb 265 – 25.07.99	12015 – 01.10.97++	04.00	E. L. Hunt
ROSE	RN 07.17	280	Bm 1359 – 13.07.17	22269 – 02.02.15	01.42	Ernest Thomas, Walsall
ROSE IN JUNE	XV 10.91		Bm 689 – 29.05.89	9391 – 14.09.94++	02.00	Union Acid Co. Ltd
ROUMANIA	SO 06.08	141	Bm 1204 – 24.07.08	20668 – 11.08.08	01.49	SED
ROVER (m)	UA 11.19	189	Uxb 516 – 28.10.19	23120 – 04.03.20	11.40	destroyed by enemy bombing
RUDD (m)	Y1 02.36	323	Bm 1582 – 21.02.36	1904 – 22.05.36	01.49	NWD
RUGBY	XF 01.89	21	Bm 767 – 24.03.91	15390 – 20.11.96	09.03	J. Brown, Sedgley
RUGBY	BK 10.13	279	Bm 1300 – 03.10.13	22735 – 12.07.17	04.33	Associated Canal Carriers Ltd
RUGELEY	UU 02.01	137	Uxb 315 – 06.02.01	22131 – 07.01.24	08.25	A. Truscott, Oxford
RUNCORN	XF 01.89		Bm 587 – 08.03.87	1396 – 20.05.90++	03.90	scrapped
RUNCORN	XW 06.89	123	Bm 870 – 04.08.93	16964 – 15.11.99	01.01	Rowley Regis Granite Co.
RUSSIA	XT 12.03	29	Bm 1124 – 12.02.04	19548 – 13.12.04	08.48	Ernest Thomas, Walsall
RUTLAND	UU 10.06	139	Uxb 413 – 27.12.06	20289 – 14.08.07	02.30	Lees & Atkins, Polesworth
SAMUEL	XP 04.90	86	Bm 770 – 14.04.91	18684 – 13.03.03	02.10	Union Acid Co. Ltd
SANDBACH	ST 11.98	159	Bm 1016 – 23.12.98	16577 – 16.02.99	07.42	Oxford Canal Company
SANDON	XF 01.89	46	Bm 712 – 14.01.90	16806 – 13.07.99	10.03	Worsey Ltd
SARDINIA	XS 12.21	147	Bm 1432 – 04.03.22	22390 – 27.09.15	02.30	Lees & Atkins, Polesworth
SARDIS	XS 08.21	224	Bm 1418 – 21.10.21	514 – 07.12.22	09.30	Lees & Atkins, Polesworth
SCOTLAND	TD 04.89	147	Wv 673 – 30.04.89	12552 – 17.10.89	05.15	William Nurser & Sons
SEAGULL (m)	UA 10.21	194	Bm 1410 – 30.09.21	1027 – 17.03.25	12.45	Ernest Thomas, Walsall
SEAGULL	XM 07.38		Wv 1084 – 10.07.22	1681 – 24.06.31	02.40	scrapped
SEAL (m)	UA 06.20	190	Bm 1390 – 02.07.20	186 – 04.03.22	01.49	SED
SEINE	XW 06.89	115	Bm 871 – 04.08.93	16272 – 01.07.98	10.99	H. B. Whitehouse
SESOSTRIS	XS 12.21	172	Bm 1441 – 30.06.22	629 – 31.03.23	12.30	Lees & Atkins, Polesworth
SETTLER	XA 07.22	131	Bm 1444 – 29.08.22	1069 – 28.07.25	03.32	Grand Union Canal Company
SHAD (m)	YI 03.36	324	Bm 1583 – 24.04.36	1905 – 22.05.36	01.49	NWD
SHAMROCK	XP 04.90	13	Bm 734 – 12.04.90	10737 – 20.12.88**	10.10	Noah Webb, Brierley Hill
SHAMROCK	XQ 02.99		Uxb 264 – 25.07.99	Not found	00.05	sold
SHANNON	XW 06.89	67	Bm 754 – 28.10.90	19711 – 13.04.05	10.10	J. Kinsey
SHARDLOW	XF 01.89	145	Bm 762 – 24.02.91	7658 – 19.05.74	09.04	J. Sheffield
SIBERIA	SO 09.08	170	Bm 1206 – 13.10.08	20805 – 14.01.09	09.38	motor boat
SIBERIA (m)	YU 09.38	345	Bm 1621 – 04.11.38	2053 – 04.01.39	01.49	NWD
SIR WM ROBERTSON	XS 08.21	208	Bm 1415 – 30.09.21	1140 – 18.02.26	09.30	Lees & Atkins, Polesworth
SKATE (m)	YI 06.36	325	Bm 1596 – 17.07.36	1984 – 01.10.37	01.49	NWD
SMETHWICK	XF 01.89		Bm 839 – 27.01.93	10851 – 28.07.96**	02.00	Sprowston
SNOWDROP	XL 06.94	18	Bm 915 – 18.01.95	16686 – 29.04.99	03.00	Abraham Lowe
SOAR	XF 01.89	105	Wv 544 – 01.06.86	16800 – 12.07.99	05.02	S. Dyehouse
SOCRATES	XS 08.21	225	Bm 1439 – 30.06.22	493 – 23.11.22	03.32	Grand Union Canal Company
SOHO	SW 04.97	210	Bm 935 – 17.04.97	16377 – 13.09.98	10.16	A. J. Harmsworth, Aldershot
SOHO	XE 12.17	249	Uxb 512 – 31.12.18	13991 – 08.06.06	06.28	scrapped
SOLIHULL	ZK 03.97	81	Bm 975 – 05.03.97	14584 – 01.10.95	03.13	Abraham Lowe
SOMERSET	LA 12.30	254	Tam 49 – 13.12.30	1668 – 01.05.31	09.46	Ernest Thomas, Walsall
SOMME	XS 08.21	226	Bm 1422 – 21.10.21	22866 – 16.05.18	03.32	Grand Union Canal Company
SPADE	XM 07.38		Wv 1128 – 14.01.29	1426 – 20.09.28	10.43	J. Dean & Sons
SPAIN	SO 06.06	140	Bm 1176 – 22.06.06	20201 – 23.04.07	01.49	SED
SPEEDWELL (s)	XW 06.89	2	Bm 648 – 08.05.88	Not found	03.94	rebuilt
SPEEDWELL (s)	SV 03.94	2	Bm 892 – 20.04.94	11676 – 30.01.11**	09.28	scrapped
SPONDON	SW 06.96	194	Bm 953 – 26.06.96	17948 – 15.10.01	10.15	Union Acid Co. Ltd
STAFFORD	ST 02.98	236	Bm 1001 – 18.03.98	16090 – 07.03.98	06.38	motor boat
STAFFORD (m)	YU 06.38	342	Bm 1617 – 17.06.38	2034 – 12.08.38	01.49	NWD
STANLEY	ZL 05.29	232	Bm 1520 – 21.06.29	1176 – 15.07.26	05.46	Ernest Thomas, Walsall
STAR	XF 01.89		Bm 605 – 14.06.87	Not found	09.04	sold
STAR	XP 04.90		Bm 731 – 22.04.90	10664 – 19.03.85**	10.99	Union Acid Co. Ltd
STAR	XE 12.17	255	Uxb 507 – 26.03.18	11729 – 07.06.10**	06.28	scrapped
STAR	XM 07.38		Wv 1133 – 08.07.29	1497 – 20.06.29	08.48	A. Warburton & Company
STOCKPORT	SW 06.95	182	Bm 938 – 25.05.95	16502 – 12.12.98	11.14	Allsopp & Sons Ltd. Burton
STOKE	XF 01.89	23	Wv 401 – 11.04.83	11011 – 17.08.82	08.05	Williams & Price
STONE	ST 07.98		Bm 1010 – 05.10.98	16341 – 25.08.98	12.41	Ernest Thomas, Walsall
STORT	XW 06.89	53	Bm 786 – 02.10.91	16965 – 15.11.99	12.04	Union Acid Co. Ltd
STOUR	XF 01.89		Not found	1396 – 20.05.90++	00.91	sold
STRETFORD	RA 04.00	71	Bm 1050 – 27.04.00	17343 – 15.08.00	12.19	Dunlop Ltd
STRUGGLER	ZM 10.89	133	Bm 768 – 24.03.91	19252 – 13.05.04	09.07	J. B. Price, Burslem
SUCCESS	XF 01.89	60	Lcr 45 – 00.00.00	16273 – 01.07.96	09.03	J. Brown, Sedgley
SUFFOLK	LA 10.30	248	Tam 96 – 18.10.30	1653 – 09.01.31	07.47	Ernest Thomas, Walsall
SULTAN (s)	SS 06.99	251	Bm 1034 – 07.07.99	11689 – 07.03.11**	05.24	motor boat
SULTAN (m)	SC 05.24	251	Bm 1540 – 15.04.32	974 – 05.12.24	12.41	Ernest Thomas, Walsall
SUNDERLAND	XW 06.89		Bm 1170 – 07.08.90	Not found	10.89	sold
SURREY	UU 03.03	91	Uxb 350 – 28.04.03	18656 – 24.06.03	07.20	T. & S. Element Ltd
SUSSEX	LA 02.26	34	Tam 13 – 13.03.26	1174 – 07.07.26	09.46	Ernest Thomas, Walsall
SWALLOW (m)	UB 07.25	24	Uxb 546 – 28.07.25	1534 – 25.11.29	01.49	SED
SWAN (ws)	UZ 03.11	257	Uxb 457 – 28.03.11	Not gauged	00.13	J. W. Winship
SWEDEN	SO 03.06	114	Bm 1170 – 16.03.06	20237 – 04.06.07	08.48	Ernest Thomas, Walsall
SWIFT (m)	UB 11.25	25	Bm 1480 – 20.11.25	1743 – 07.10.32	01.49	SED
SWINDON	XF 01.89	153	Bm 861 – 16.06.93	17452 – 05.10.00	05.10	H. Mills, Pensnett
SYDNEY	XF 01.89		Wv 435 – 15.04.84	16748 – 16.06.99	10.99	Union Acid Co. Ltd
SYLVIA (w)	XN 11.89		Lon 186 – 13.02.90	Not found	08.94	Tough & Henderson
SYSTON	ZN 05.96	200	Bm 956 – 31.07.96	18499 – 05.03.03	09.12	Isaac Slater, Alrewas
TAME	XW 06.89	29	Bm 824 – 13.10.92	11004 – 03.08.82	01.04	Union Acid Co. Ltd
TASMANIA	SO 10.08	171	Bm 1209 – 01.01.09	21000 – 13.12.09	07.42	Oxford Canal Company
TAURUS	XM 07.38	348	Mx 24 – 26.09.27	1323 – 02.09.27	01.49	NWD
TEAK	UT 01.01	122	Uxb 310 – 29.01.01	18188 – 29.05.02	08.27	Harry Canvin, Leckhamstead
TEES	XF 01.89	39	Bm 799 – 29.01.82	19335 – 05.07.04	11.07	Derby Cooperative Society
TEME	XW 06.89	114	Bm 833 – 17.12.92	12425 – 04.05.89	01.04	Union Acid Co. Ltd
TENCH (m)	YI 09.36	326	Bm 1600 – 16.10.36	1962 – 11.06.37	01.49	NWD
THE KING (s)	SS 04.05	103	Bm 1152 – 05.05.05	11681 – 13.02.11**	06.25	motor boat
THISTLE	XQ 02.99	247	Uxb 261 – 30.05.99	17821 – 11.07.01	04.16	H. J. Chapman
TIBER	XW 06.89	11	Bm 834 – 17.12.92	17165 – 12.04.00	09.03	J. Brown, Sedgley
TIPTON	SW 04.97	209	Bm 978 – 02.04.97	18659 – 25.06.03	09.16	A. J. Harmsworth, Aldershot
TITANIA	XS 12.21	142	Bm 1431 – 25.02.22	21334 – 19.07.11	02.30	Lees & Atkins, Polesworth
TIVIDALE	UU 01.11	230	Uxb 455 – 31.01.11	1139 – 18.02.26	03.31	Charles Ward
TORQUAY	XF 01.89		Bm 725 – 22.04.90	10762 – 09.05.90**	05.98	Union Acid Co. Ltd
TRAVELLER	XF 01.89		Wv 223 – 08.04.79	1396 – 20.05.90++	00.91	sold
TRENT (w)	XX 12.96		Uxb 497 – 28.09.15	9275 – 01.01.97++	04.25	Alfred Buck & Son, Brentford
TRENT (w)	RE 05.97		Lcr 99 – 08.05.97	Not gauged	06.09	sold
TRENTHAM	XF 01.89	62	Bm 722 – 11.03.90	19235 – 10.05.04	01.06	sold
TRING	XF 01.89	51	Bm 579 – 15.03.87	12101 – 22.09.87	00.02	J. E. Perry & Son
TRING	RN 11.14	138	Bm 1324 – 18.12.14	20390 – 17.10.07	01.49	SED
TROUT (m)	YI 09.36	327	Bm 1599 – 16.10.36	1986 – 20.10.37	01.49	NWD
TUNSTALL	UU 12.99	60	Uxb 277 – 30.01.00	17149 – 04.04.00	10.16	A. J. Harmsworth, Aldershot
TURKEY	SO 11.06	138	Bm 1184 – 30.11.06	20390 – 17.10.07	11.14	renamed "Tring"
TWEED	XW 06.89		Bm 750 – 08.07.90	6464 – 25.02.74	12.99	Slater & Company
TWO SISTERS	XP 06.97	176	Lon 362 – 29.10.00	16366 – 08.09.98	03.13	Bradley Steel Strip Company

TWYFORD	ST 05.00	61	Bm 1051 – 18.05.00	17685 – 20.04.01	11.42 Wheeldon Sanitary Potteries
TYNE	XW 06.89		Bm 757 – 11.11.90	17719 – 14.05.01	02.02 Union Acid Co. Ltd
UNA	XG 12.89		Wv 627 – 26.06.88	9415 – 14.09.94++	00.07 sold
UNA	UG 12.11	205	Uxb 464 – 28.12.11	21703 – 30.01.13	03.32 Grand Union Canal Company
UPTON	UU 11.11	223	Uxb 463 – 28.12.11	22018 – 28.02.14	03.32 Grand Union Canal Company
UPWOOD	BK 03.14	283	Bm 1311 – 20.03.14	22209 – 23.10.14	01.49 SED
URMSTON	BK 01.14	282	Bm 1309 – 30.01.14	22202 – 15.10.14	01.49 NWD
USK	XW 06.89	33	Bm 867 – 14.07.93	11288 – 06.10.83	01.07 J. B. Price, Burslem
USK	WO 11.11	218	Bm 1215 – 24.11.11	21896 – 25.10.13	12.29 Grand Union Canal Company
UXBRIDGE	UU 06.97	213	Uxb 221 – 00.06.97	17831 – 19.07.01	11.15 Cadbury Brothers Ltd
UXBRIDGE	UU 09.31	208	Uxb 577 – 29.09.31	12532 – 18.06.36**	01.49 SED
VANGUARD (s)	SS 07.11	214	Bm 1243 – 29.09.11	11895 – 21.06.16**	11.26 motor boat
VANGUARD (m)	SC 11.26	214	Bm 1550 – 25.05.34	11895 – 21.06.16**	01.49 SED
VENICE	SO 12.10	199	Bm 1229 – 27.01.11	22045 – 24.03.14	01.49 NWD
VENUS	XM 07.38		Wv 1140 – 14.03.32	550 – 17.01.23	06.41 Ernest Thomas, Walsall
VERBENA	RN 06.16	203	Bm 1347 – 23.06.16	22624 – 01.03.17	10.42 G. Mellor & Co. Ltd
VERBENA	XF 01.89		Bm 840 – 27.01.93	9417 – 14.09.94++	09.01 J. E. Perry & Son
VICEROY (s)	SS 12.09	196	Bm 1214 – 03.12.09	11695 – 03.04.11**	11.27 motor boat
VICEROY (m)	SC 11.27	196	Bm 1544 – 24.02.33	1394 – 08.05.28	08.48 Ernest Thomas, Walsall
VICTORIA (w)	XF 01.89		Lon 49 – 17.12.87	9434 – 14.09.94++	01.00 Thames Steam Tug
VICTORIA	XF 01.89		Bm 884 – 27.10.93	1396 – 20.05.90++	05.98 sold
VICTORIA (s)	XW 06.89	117	Bm 848 – 23.03.93	12720 – 15.04.90	07.19 scrapped
VICTORY	XW 06.89		Bm 744 – 03.06.90	10613 – 06.03.83**	10.92 sold
VICTORY	XC 10.93		Bm 880 – 27.10.93	9418 – 14.09.94++	12.01 sold
VICTORY (s)	SS 08.11	216	Bm 1247 – 15.12.11	Not gauged	09.27 motor boat
VICTORY (m)	SC 09.27	216	Bm 1622 – 16.12.38	1351 – 09.11.27	10.46 J. Dean & Sons
VIENNA	SO 02.11	203	Bm 1234 – 03.03.11	11821 – 19.04.12**	06.16 renamed "Verbena"
VIOLET	XL 06.94	94	Bm 914 – 21.12.94	18578 – 01.05.03	04.08 Union Acid Co. Ltd
VIOLET	RD 05.16	98	Lcr 137 – 23.06.16	625 – 23.03.23	09.30 Lees & Atkins, Polesworth
VULCAN (g)	SE 11.06	183	Bm 1207 – 27.11.08	Not gauged	11.10 steamer
VULCAN (s)	SR 11.10	183	Bm 1226 – 25.11.10	11690 – 20.03.11**	09.27 motor boat
VULCAN (m)	SC 09.27	183	Bm 1538 – 15.04.32	2167 – 11.08.43	09.47 Ernest Thomas, Walsall
WALES	SW 06.94	172	Bm 902 – 20.07.94	16584 – 22.02.99	03.15 Union Acid Co. Ltd
WALNUT	UT 02.01	123	Uxb 313 – 26.02.01	17684 – 19.04.01	01.23 scrapped
WALSALL	UU 01.11	229	Uxb 454 – 31.01.11	996 – 16.01.25	03.32 Grand Union Canal Company
WALTER (w)	XX 11.94		Not 127 – 08.03.95	Not gauged	00.00 not known
WARWICK	SW 04.96	189	Bm 950 – 17.04.96	16620 – 14.03.99	08.15 Allsopp & Sons Ltd., Burton
WATFORD	SW 05.95	179	Bm 936 – 03.05.95	15901 – 02.11.97	04.26 Erewash Canal Company
WEAVER	XF 01.89	121	Bm 747 – 24.06.90	19554 – 16.12.04	03.09 Adolphe Crosbie Ltd
WEAVER	XG 12.89	103	Bm 758 – 25.11.90	17484 – 18.10.00	10.03 sold
WEDNESBURY	XF 01.89		Bm 662 – 25.09.88	1396 – 20.05.90++	04.94 William Hunt & Sons
WEDNESBURY	SW 04.94	52	Bm 895 – 20.04.94	19909 – 05.12.05	05.15 William Nurser & Sons
WEEDON	XF 01.89		Bm 743 – 03.06.90	9424 – 14.09.94++	10.99 Union Acid Co. Ltd
WELLWISHER	XS 08.21	227	Bm 1416 – 21.10.21	22834 – 26.04.18	03.32 Grand Union Canal Company
WELTON	XP 06.97	175	Uxb 242 – 16.09.98	19771 – 03.06.05	01.11 S. W. B. Stephen, Smethwick
WESSEX	LA 12.25	28	Tam 7 – 16.01.26	1142 – 26.02.26	03.41 Imperial Chemical Industries Ltd
WHISPERER	XS 08.21	228	Bm 1417 – 21.10.21	22762 – 11.09.17	03.32 Grand Union Canal Company
WILD ROSE (ws)	ZO 08.21		Oxf 54 – 02.01.89	1014 – 23.03.89++	00.00 sold
WILLIAM	XP 04.90		Bm 791 – 16.10.91	12763 – 04.06.90	06.00 sold
WILLOW	XS 08.21	231	Bm 1426 – 21.10.21	977 – 11.12.24	12.30 Lees & Atkins, Polesworth
WINDSOR	XF 01.89	112	Bm 844 – 04.03.93	19785 – 24.06.05	10.08 Union Acid Co. Ltd
WINSFORD	ST 06.98	239	Bm 1007 – 03.06.98	16543 – 19.01.99	06.46 Ernest Thomas, Walsall
WISDOM	XS 08.21	233	Bm 1420 – 21.10.21	583 – 06.02.23	03.32 Grand Union Canal Company
WOBBY	WE 06.99	23	Ber 284 – 07.06.99	18210 – 06.06.02	04.16 Anchor Iron & Steel Company
WOLLATON	SW 12.96	49	Bm 965 – 05.01.97	19319 – 28.06.04	02.18 Forrester Clayton, Brentford
WOLVERTON	UU 06.98	70	Uxb 245 – 25.10.98	16368 – 09.09.98	05.22 scrapped
WORSLEY	XF 01.89	139	Bm 760 – 27.01.91	13026 – 01.06.91	10.04 J. Allen, Wolvercote
WYE	XF 01.89		Bm 645 – 24.04.88	11844 – 15.01.86	12.99 Slater & Company
WYKEN	XQ 10.98		Uxb 249 – 25.10.98	Not found	00.00 not known
YARDLEY	ST 07.11	212	Bm 1239 – 07.07.11	22338 – 24.06.15	01.49 SED
YARMOUTH	BK 04.14	284	Bm 1313 – 01.05.14	22271 – 08.02.15	11.42 Samuel Barlow Coal Co. Ltd
YEADING	ST 01.12	235	Bm 1250 – 29.12.11	23121 – 04.03.20	01.49 SED
YIEWSLEY	ST 03.12	167	Bm 1253 – 16.02.12	23135 – 26.03.20	01.49 SED
YORK	ST 07.12	112	Bm 1263 – 09.07.12	21977 – 30.01.14	01.49 SED
YPRES	XS 08.21	234	Bm 1414 – 30.09.21	992 – 02.01.25	12.30 Lees & Atkins, Polesworth
7 (d)	BL 10.00	7	Not registered	17464 – 11.10.00	00.00 Birmingham Electricity Dept
9 (d)	XX 11.16	9	Not registered	22596 – 18.11.16	04.26 Birmingham coke boat
25 (d)	XX 05.01	25	Not registered	17724 – 25.05.01	00.00 Birmingham Electricity Dept
28 (d)	XX 11.04	28	Not registered	19531 – 22.11.04	05.12 scrapped
98 (d)	BL 11.98	98	Not registered	16470 – 21.11.98	00.00 Birmingham Electricity Dept
134 (d)	XX 06.95	134	Not registered	14363 – 20.06.95	00.00 scrapped
134 (d)	BL 08.01	134	Not registered	17881 – 31.08.01	00.00 H. H. Vivian & Co. Ltd
187 (d)	BL 11.98	187	Not registered	14879 – 29.02.96	00.00 scrapped

NOTES:

The fleet list has been based on the company's docking book supplemented by information from canal boat registers, gauging and other records. Whilst the docking book is fairly comprehensive from 1900 onwards, it only covers details of some of the earlier craft and particularly those that made up the initial fleet meaning there may well be inaccuracies in this area.

KEY TO TYPE:

(d) – day boat: (g) – gas boat: (m) – motorboat: (o) – open boat: (s) – steamer: (w) – wide boat

KEY TO REGISTRATIONS

Bm – Birmingham	ByH – Brierley Hill	Ber – Berkhamsted	Ilk – Ilkeston
Lcr – Leicester	Lon – London (Port of)	Not – Nottingham	Oxf – Oxford
Pad – Paddington	Tam – Tamworth	Uxb – Uxbridge	War – Warwick
Wv – Wolverhampton			

KEY TO FATES:

NWD – North Western Division of the Docks & Inland Waterways Executive
SED – South Eastern Division of the Docks & Inland Waterways Executive

NOTE RE GAUGINGS:

Most of the gaugings are from the Birmingham Canal Navigations, but these are only complete from 1895 onwards. Where no BCN gauging could be found, but one exists for the Grand Junction Canal, this has been included marked with a double asterisk (**).

Likewise several boats were gauged for the Thames Watermen's Hall and these are marked with a double cross (++). In the early days these were all recorded under FMC's number (1396), but from 1894 boats were awarded their own individual numbers.

FLEET NUMBERS:

In 1937/8 three fleet numbers were duplicated – HOLLAND 339, ARABIA 340 and GAILEY 341. Later these boats reverted to the numbers they had held before being converted to motorboats.

KEY TO BOATS ENTERING THE FLEET

SALTLEY DOCK – FELLOWS, MORTON & CLAYTON LTD

SC	Iron composite steamers converted to motors (20 – see list)
SD	Wooden steamers converted to motors (*Duteous, Hecla*)
SE	Iron composite gas-engine boat (*Vulcan*)
SG	Girl Class wooden butties (*Daisy, Hettie, Maud, May, Nancy*)
SM	Iron composite motors (*Lapwing, Lark, Laurel, Leopard, Lily, Linda, Lion. Lotus, Lupin, Lynx*)
SN	2nd batch iron composites motors (*Peacock, Petrel, Penguin, Plover*)
SO	Overseas Class iron composite butties (30 – see list)
SP	Steamer rebuilt from steel to wood (*Duke*)
SR	Iron composite gas boat converted to steamer (*Vulcan*)
SS	Iron composite steamers (16 – see list)
ST	Town Class iron composite butties (34 – see list)
SU	Wooden steamer (*Earl*)
SV	Wooden steamers rebuilt (*Phoenix, Pirate, Speedwell*)
SW	Town Class wooden butties (30 – see list)
SX	Steamers rebuilt from steel to iron composite (*Countess, Empress, Princess*)

UXBRIDGE DOCK – FELLOWS, MORTON & CLAYTON LTD

UA	1st batch of wooden motors (*Lindola, Quail, Rambler, Raven, Robin, Rover, Seagull, Seal*)
UB	2nd batch of wooden motors (*Swallow, Swift*)
UC	3rd batch of wooden motors (*Aster, Azalea*)
UD	4th batch of wooden motors (*Beech, Begonia, Briar, Daffodil, Dahlia, Elder, Erica*)
UF	5th batch of wooden motors (Fish Class – *Brill, Carp*)
UG	Girl Class wooden butties (30 – see list))
UH	6th batch of wooden motors (Hill Class – *Chiltern, Clee, Clent, Cotswold*)
UO	Overseas Class wooden butty (*Java*)
UR	River Class wooden butties (*Aire, Anker, Clyde, Conway, Dart, Dee, Evenlode, Exe*)
US	Wooden steamers (*Hecla, Duteous*)
UT	Tree Class wooden butties built by A J Ash at the dock (20 – see list)
UU	Town Class wooden butties (37 – see list)
UV	Wooden wide craft (*Apsley, Braunston, Croxley, Harefield, Isleworth, Islington*)
UW	Wooden wide motor boat (*Pioneer*)
UX	Wooden motor boats rebuilt (*Quail, Rambler, Raven*)
UZ	Wooden wide steamer (*Swan*)

NORTHWICH YARD – W J YARWOOD & SONS LIMITED

YA	1st batch iron composite motor boats (12 – see list)
YB	2nd batch iron-composite hulls fitted out Saltley (*Eagle, Elk, Emu, Falcon, Ferret, Greyhound, Hare, Ibex*)
YC	2nd batch iron-comp hulls fitted out Uxbridge (*Fox, Hawk, Jackal, Jaguar*)
YD	3rd batch iron-comp motors (*Kangaroo, Kestrel, Nautilus, Ostrich, Otter, Owl*)
YE	4th batch iron-comp hulls fitted out Saltley (*Panther*)
YF	4th batch iron-comp hulls fitted out Uxbridge (*Python*)
YG	5th batch coppered-steel hulls fitted out Saltley (*Acacia, Alder, Apple*)
YH	6th batch coppered-steel Fish Class hulls fitted out Saltley (*Bream, Chub; Dace, Dory*)
YI	6th batch coppered steel Fish Class hulls fitted out Saltley (12 – see list)
YJ	7th batch iron composite hulls fitted out Saltley (*Cactus, Clematis, Clover, Cypress*)
YK	7th batch coppered-steel hulls fitted out Uxbridge (*Bramble*)
YL	Final batch coppered-steel hulls fitted out Saltley (*Fern, Foxglove, Gardenia, Gorse*)
YM	Coppered-steel Hill Class hulls fitted out Saltley (*Malvern, Mendip*)

YU	Iron composite craft converted to motors, fitted out Saltley (12 – see list)

OTHER BUILDERS (in wood unless stated otherwise)

BK	Braithwaite & Kirk, West Bromwich Dock (24 iron composite craft – see list)
BL	Braithwaite & Kirk, West Bromwich Dock (4 iron day boats) (*7, 98, 134, 137*)
HA	Harris, Netherton (iron composite craft) (*Madeley, Malvern*)
LA	Lees & Atkins, Polesworth, (*Cornwall, Essex, Middlesex, Norfolk, Somerset, Suffolk, Sussex, Wessex*)
NB	Nurser Brothers, Braunston (*Bascote*)
PE	Sephton Brothers, Polesworth Dock (*Dorset*)
RA	Rathbone Brothers, Stretford (*Chelford, Moore, Stretford*)
RD	Rudkin Brothers, Leicester Dock (*Belgrave, Frank, Radford, Violet*)
RE	Rudkin Brothers, Leicester Dock (wide boats) (*Aylestone, Trent*)
TD	Fellows Morton & Clayton Ltd., Tipton Dock (*Scotland*)
WE	W. E. Costin Ltd, Berkhamsted Dock (*Merioneth, Montgomery, Polly, Wobby*)
WN	William Nurser & Sons, Braunston (*Emscote*)
WO	Worsey Ltd (*Usk*)

KEY TO PURCHASES FROM OTHER CARRIERS

XA	S Allsopp & Sons Ltd, Burton on Trent (*Banker, Pioneer, Settler*
XB	Ellen Hughes, trading as Hugh Hughes, Brentford (*Ealing, Hayes, Lily*)
XC	Cudlipp & Sons, Little Eaton, Derby (*Forward, Guildford, Richmond, Victory*)
XD	London & Birmingham Canal Carrying Co Ltd (16 boats – see list)
XE	W. & S. Foster (1912) Ltd, Tipton (*Bersham, Clent, Nantwich, Soho, Star*)
XF	Fellows Morton & Company (94 boats – see list)
XG	Fanshaw & Pinson, Wolverhampton (13 boats – see list)
XH	John Dickinson & Co. Ltd, Apsley Mill (*Chester, Lichfield*)
XI	George Hurst & Sons, Northampton & Leighton Buzzard (*Dauntless, Primrose, Roach*)
XL	Alfred S. Landon, City Road Basin (Bluebell, *Forget Me Not, Snowdrop, Violet*)
XM	Midland & Coast Canal Carriers Ltd, Wolverhampton (16 boats – see list)
XN	Nash & Miller, Battersea (*Cairo, Egypt, Lurline, Pearl, Sylvia*)
XP	Samuel Phipkin, Hillingdon (30 boats – see list)
XQ	Phipkin & Palmer, Yiewsley (*Exhall, Hawkesbury, Iver, Ivinghoe, Longford, Shamrock, Thistle, Wyken*)
XS	Shropshire Union Railways & Canal Company, Chester (25 boats – see list)
XT	Thomas Clayton (Oldbury) Ltd, Oldbury (*Beaver, Japan, Russia*)
XU	Thomas Clayton (Paddington) Ltd, Paddington (*Majestic, Ouse*)
XV	William Hunt & Sons, Wednesbury (*Plover, Rose in June*)
XW	William Clayton, Saltley (32 boats – see list)
XX	Previous builders/owners not known

SINGLE ACQUISITIONS

ZA	John Bradshaw, Birmingham (*Ampliss Mary*)
ZB	John Whalley, Stoke on Trent (*Avon*)
ZC	John Hambridge (virtually a new boat by Sephtons) (*Devon*)
ZD	John Dormer Kendall (*Dreadnought*)
ZE	R. Furley & Company, Gainsborough (*Elizabeth*)
ZF	John Wilkins (*Fanny*)
ZG	Proctor & Ryland, Birmingham (*Hannah*)
ZH	Enoch A Whitehouse (virtually a new boat by Rudkins) (*Leicester*)
ZI	Odell & Company, Paddington (*Norwood*)
ZJ	Hoskins & Sewell, Birmingham (*Otter*)
ZK	William Stokes, Brierley Hill (*Solihull*)

ZL   Cadbury Brothers Ltd., Bournville (*Stanley*)
ZM   Reuben Harris, Oldbury (*Struggler*)
ZN   Davies & Son (*Syston*)
ZO   Oxford & London Steam Tug Company (*Wild Rose*)

RENAMED BOATS

ACTON (07.15 ex Middlesex)
AMESBURY (11.14 ex AUSTRIA)
ENGLAND (08.14 ex GERMANY)
KERRY (08.13 ex KINGSTOWN)
ROSE (07.17 ex RHINE)
TRING (11.14 ex TURKEY)
VERBENA (06.16 ex VIENNA)

DETAILS OF LARGER ACQUISITIONS

SALTLEY DOCK

SC (20 iron composite steamers converted to motor boats): ADMIRAL 06.24; BARON 02.15; BRITON (ex BARONESS) 05.15; CAPTAIN (ex COUNTESS) 07.24; COLONEL 09.24; COUNT 07.25; EMPEROR 04.17; ENVOY (ex EMPRESS) 10.19; GENERAL 05.24; KING (ex THE KING) 06.25; MARQUIS 03.25; MONARCH 01.25; PILOT (ex PRINCESS) 12.24; PRESIDENT 05.25; PRINCE 03.26; SULTAN 05.24; VANGUARD 11.26; VICEROY 11.27; VICTORY 09.27; VULCAN 09.27.

SO (30 Overseas Class iron composite butties) ARABIA 02.07; AUSTRIA 06.05; AUSTRALIA 07.94; BELGIUM 08.05; COLUMBIA 05.07; DENMARK 09.05; DURBAN 07.03; EGYPT 11.03; FRANCE 08.04; GAMBIA 06.07; GERMANY 11.04; HOLLAND 12.05; INDIA 12.03; ITALY 04.05; JERSEY 04.10; KIMBERLEY 03.03; NATAL 10.03; NORWAY 01.06; PERSIA 03.08; PORTUGAL 06.06; PRETORIA 01.03; QUEBEC 09.10; ROUMANIA 06.08; SIBERIA 08.09; SPAIN 06.06; SWEDEN 03.06; TASMANIA 10.08; TURKEY 11.06; VENICE 12.10; VIENNA 02.11.

SS (16 iron composite steamers): ADMIRAL 09.05; BARON 11.98; BARONESS 11.98; COLONEL 06.99; COUNT 06.99; EMPEROR 05.98; GENERAL 11.07; MARQUIS 03.98; MONARCH 04.08; PRESIDENT 06.09; PRINCE 10.98; SULTAN 06.99; THE KING 04.05; VANGUARD 07.11; VICEROY 12.09; VICTORY 08.11.

ST (34 Town Class iron composite boats): BULBOURNE 03.98; BURSLEM 08.98; DAWLEY 04.99; DRAYTON 05.99; FAZELEY 08.21; FORWARD 06.22; FOXTON 05.00; GAILEY 10.99; GLASGOW 02.09; GRIMSBY 03.10; HANLEY 01.99; HANWELL 04.00; HARECASTLE 02.99; HARTFORD 12.98; IPSWICH 04.12; IVER 07.12; KEGWORTH 07.10; KESWICK 11.10; KILBURN 05.10; LEIGHTON 01.98; LONGTON 10.98; NORTHOLT 12.99; NORTHWICH 12.98; OLDBURY 02.00; PENKRIDGE 01.98; SANDBACH 11.98; STAFFORD 02.98; STONE 07.98; TWYFORD 05.00; WINSFORD 06.98; YARDLEY 07.11; YEADING 01.12; YIEWSLEY 03.12; YORK 07.12.

SW (30 Town Class wooden butties): ANGLESEY 02.03; ASHTON 05.95; BELFAST 03.95; BOXMOOR 03.95; BRECON 03.03; BRENTFORD 12.02; BURTON 10.96; DAVENTRY 06.94; DENBIGH 12.05; DERBY 07.96; DIGBY 06.97; DUDLEY 06.97; FLINT 01.06; HATTON 03.06; HOCKLEY 04.97; HYDE 07.95; KINGSWOOD 02.01; KNOWLE 06.96; LEAMINGTON 04.96; MARPLE 06.95; NETHERTON 01.97; SOHO 04.97; SPONDON 06.96; STOCKPORT 06.95; TIPTON 04.97; WALES 06.94; WARWICK 04.96; WATFORD 03.95; WEDNESBURY 04.94; WOLLATON 12.96.

UXBRIDGE DOCK

UG (30 Girl Class wooden butties): ADA 07.22; ALICE 03.10; AMY 09.22; BEATRICE 10.22; BESSIE 12.22; CLARA 04.23; CONSTANCE 01.23; DILYS 06.23; DOROTHY 07.23; EDITH 02.26; ELSIE 04.26; ENA 08.26; EVEYLYN 03.27; FANNY 07.27; FAY 11.27; FLORENCE 01.28; FREDA 04.28;

GERTIE 07.28; GLADYS 12.28; GRACE 03.29; GRETA 08.29; HELEN 06.30; HETTIE 03.30; HILDA 12.29; IDA 12.30; IRENE 04.31; IVY 02.32; JOAN 02.33; KATE 05.10; UNA 12.11.

UT (20 Tree Class wooden butties): APPLE 01.00; ASH 01.00; BEECH 03.00; BIRCH 03.00; CEDAR 04.00; CHESTNUT 04.00; EBONY 05.00; ELM 05.00; FIR 07.00; IVY 07.00; LARCH 07.00; LEMON 09.00; MAPLE 09.00; OAK 10.00; ORANGE 11.00; PEAR 12.00; PINE 11.00; POPLAR 01.01; TEAK 01.01; WALNUT 02.01.

UU (37 Town Class wooden butties): AYLESBURY 01.98; BARTON 10.99; BUCKBY 06.99; BUCKINGHAM 06.98; CAERNARVON 01.06; CARDIGAN 01.06; CHESHIRE 03.99; COLWICH 01.08; COWLEY 03.98; CREWE 03.99; DENHAM 06.98; ELLESMERE 01.07; ETRURIA 09.99; FENNY 01.98; FRADLEY 03.01; JARROW 04.12; LANCASTER 01.07; LANGLEY 05.98; MARSWORTH 05.98; MIDDLESEX 01.03; MONMOUTH 05.06; NAPTON 06.99; OLTON 01.00; PEMBROKE 03.06; PRESTON 09.08; RADNOR 03.06; ROCHDALE 02.08; RUGELEY 02.01; RUTLAND 10.06; SURREY 03.03; TIVIDALE 01.11; TUNSTALL 12.99; UPTON 11.11; UXBRIDGE 06.97; UXBRIDGE 09.31; WALSALL 01.11; WOLVERTON 06.98.

YARWOODS

YA (Initial batch of 12 iron composite motor boats) ADDER 04.23; ANTELOPE 06.23; AVIS (ALLIGATOR) 06.23; BADGER 06.23; BISON 12.23; BUFFALO (01.24); CAMEL 04.24; CORMORANT 04.24; CRANE (CROCODILE) 10.24; DOLPHIN 09.24; DRAGON 01.25.

YI (12 Fish Class iron composite hulls): LAMPREY 08.34; LING 10.24; MINNOW 12.34; MULLET 12.34; PERCH 03.35; PIKE 04.35; ROACH 12.35; RUDD 02.36; SHAD 03.36; SKATE 06.36; TENCH 09.36; TROUT 09.36.

YU (12 iron composite butty conversions to motors) ARABIA 07.37; COLUMBIA 01.39; ENGLAND 02.38; FRANCE 05.37; GAILEY 08.37; GAMBIA 08.38; HANLEY 07.38; HOLLAND 06.37; KIMBERLEY 05.38; PORTUGAL 10.37; SIBERIA 09.38; STAFFORD 06.38.

BRAITHWAITE & KIRK

BK (24 iron composite butties): GRANGE 05.12; GRANTHAM 06.12; GRAVESEND 06.12; GREET 06.12; GOOLE 07.12; GOSPORT 07.12; HAMPTON 08.12; HEREFORD 06.12; ILFORD 09.12; ILKESTON 09.12; JAMES 10.12; JOHN 12.12; KIDSGROVE 02.13; KILDARE 03.13; KILSBY 04.13; KINETON 05.13; KINGSBURY 06.13; KINGSTOWN 08.13; RHINE 11.13; ROMFORD 12.13; RUGBY 10.13; UPWOOD 03.14; URMSTON 01.14; YARMOUTH 04.14.

ACQUISITIONS FROM OTHER CARRIERS

LONDON & BIRMINGHAM CANAL CARRYING CO. LTD

XD: (17 boats) July 1898: ASTER, BUTTERCUP, COWSLIP, DAFFODIL, EUTOCA, FUSCHIA, GERANIUM, HONESTY, IRIS, JUNIPER, KINGCUP, LILAC, MAYFLOWER, MYRTLE, NETTLE, OLIVE, PANSY.

FELLOWS MORTON & COMPANY

XF: (95 boats) January 1889: AFRICA, ALBION, ALEXANDER, ALICE (w), AMERICA, ARTHUR, ASIA, AVON, BALACLAVA, BARLASTON, BELFAST, BILSTON, BOADICEA, BOMBAY, BRENTFORD, CALCUTTA, CAMELIA, CEYLON, CHINA, CLYDE, COMET, COVENTRY, CRICK, DAVENTRY, DERWENT, DOVE, DUCHESS (s), DUKE (s), EDEN, ELIZABETH, EMMA, EMPRESS (s), ENGLAND, EUROPE, EXPERIMENT, FIDGET, FREDERICK, GAINSBORO, GANGES, GRAVESEND, GREAT BRIDGE, HANDSWORTH, HATHERTON, HECLA (s), HETTIE, HOPE, IRELAND, ITALY, LAURETTA, LEAM, LEICESTER, LIVERPOOL, LOUISA (w), LUDLOW, MADRAS, MANCHESTER, MARIA, MURIEL, NELSON, OXFORD, PENDLETON, PERSEVERANCE, PHOENIX (s), PLYMOUTH, PRESTON, PRINCESS (s), PROSPEROUS, QUEEN (s), RUGBY, RUNCORN, SANDON, SHARDLOW, SMETHWICK, SOAR, STAR, STOKE, STOUR, SUCCESS, SWINDON, SYDNEY, TEES, TORQUAY, TRAVELLER, TRENTHAM,

TRING, VERBENA, VICTORIA (w), VICTORIA, WEAVER, WEDNESBURY, WEEDON, WINDSOR, WORSLEY, WYE, together with COUNTESS (s)– under construction.

FANSHAW & PINSON

XG: (13boats) December 1889: DON, ELK, FINCHFIELD, GEORGE, HAPPY RETURN, LEO, LIBERTY, PIONEER, PRINCESS, REX, ROE, UNA, WEAVER.

MIDLANDS & COAST CANAL CARRIERS LIMITED

XM: (July 1938) 4 motors: APOLLO, ARIEL, JUBILEE, POLE STAR. 12 butties: DIAMOND, JUPITER, MARGARET, MERCURY, MERMAID, NEPTUNE, ORION, SEAGULL, SPADE, STAR, TAURUS, VENUS.

SAMUEL PHIPKIN

XP: (15 boats in first batch and 18 in second) April 1890: ALEXANDRA, ARTHUR, ELIZABETH, EMILY, JANE, JOHN, JOSEPH, LIFFEY, LILY, MARGARET, OUSE, SAMUEL, SHAMROCK, STAR, WILLIAM. June 1897: ANNIE, BLISWORTH (w), BRAUNSTON, COSGROVE, DAUNTLESS, EDITH, EMMA, EMILY (w), GAYTON, INDUSTRY, JAMES, LINFORD, LINSLADE, NORTON, PHOEBE (w), ROSE, TWO SISTERS, WELTON.

SHROPSHIRE UNION RAILWAYS & CANAL COMPANY

XS::(20 boats in first batch and 5 in the second) August 1921: ALBERT, ARRAS, BLACKCOCK, BRIGADIER, CLEOPATRA, CRACOW, CROWN, DELVILLE, MUNITION, OPHELIA, OTHELLO, SARDIS, SIR WILLIAM ROBERTSON, SOCRATES, SOMME, WELLWISHER, WHISPERER, WILLOW, WISDOM, YPRES. December 1921: FAIRYFIELD, IMOGEN, SARDINIA, SESOSTRIS, TITANIA.

WILLIAM CLAYTON

XW: (33 boats) June 1889: ANKER, ARROW, BIRKENHEAD, COLE, DEE, EXCELSIOR, HUMBER, ISIS, LARK, LEA, LIVERPOOL, MEDWAY, MERSEY, NENE, NILE, OHIO, PIRATE (s), RHINE, RIBBLE, RUNCORN, SEINE, SHANNON, SPEEDWELL (s), STORT, SUNDERLAND, TAME, TEME, TIBER, TWEED, TYNE, USK, VICTORIA (s), VICTORY.

DETAILS OF LARGER DISPOSALS

GRAND UNION CANAL COMPANY

19 boats: ALBERT 03.32, FRANK 03.32, JARROW 03.32, JAVA 03.32, MUNITION 03.32; OPHELIA 03.32; OTHELLO 03.32; PRESTON 02.29; RADFORD 03.32; SETTLER 03.32; SOCRATES 03.32, SOMME 03.32, UNA 03.32, UPTON 03.32, USK 12.29, WALSALL 03.32, WELLWISHER 03.32, WHISPERER 03.32; WISDOM 03.32.

LEES & ATKINS, POLESWORTH

21 boats: ARRAS 09.30, BRECON 02.30, BRIGADIER 09.30, CLEOPATRA 09.30, CRACOW 09.30, DELVILLE 09.30, ELLESMERE 02.30, LANCASTER 02.30, PEAR 09.30, PINE 09.30, PIONEER 07.42, RADNOR 02.30, RUTLAND 02.30, SARDINIA 02.30, SARDIS 09.30, SESOSTRIS 12.30, SIR WILLIAM ROBERTSON 09.30, TITANIA 02.30, VIOLET 09.30, WILLOW 12.30, YPRES 12.30.

NORTH WESTERN DIVISION, DOCKS & INLAND WATERWAYS EXECUTIVE

54 motors: January 1949: ACACIA, ADDER, ALDER, APPLE, ARABIA, ARIEL, AVIS, BADGER, BREAM, BRILL, CARP, CHILTERN, CHUB, CLEE, CLEMATIS, CLENT, COLUMBIA, CORMORANT, CYPRESS, DACE, DOLPHIN, DORY, DRAGON, EAGLE, ELK, ENGLAND, FERRET, FRANCE, GAILEY, GAMBIA, HANLEY, HOLLAND, KANGAROO, KIMBERLEY, LAMPREY, LAPWING, LING, MINNOW, MULLET, OTTER, PERCH, PIKE, PORTUGAL, ROACH, RUDD, SHAD, SIBERIA, SKATE, STAFFORD, TENCH, TROUT & after nationalisation GORSE 03.51, MALVERN 09.49, MENDIP 10.49.

13 butties: January 1949: FOXTON, HANWELL, HILDA, IPSWICH, IRENE, IVY, JOHN, MADELEY, NORTHWICH, PERSIA, TAURUS, URMSTON, VENICE.

SOUTH EASTERN DIVISION, DOCKS & INLAND WATERWAYS EXECUTIVE

56 motors: January 1949: ANTELOPE, ASTER, AZALEA, BEECH, BEGONIA, BISON, BRAMBLE, BRIAR, BUFFALO, CACTUS, CAMEL, CLOVER, CRANE, DAFFODIL, DAHLIA, DOVE, ELDER, EMU, ERICA, FALCON, FERN, FOX, FOXGLOVE, GARDENIA, GREYHOUND, HARE, HAWK, IBEX, JACKAL, JAGUAR, KESTREL, LARK, LAUREL, LEOPARD, LILY, LINDA, LION, LOTUS, LUPIN, LYNX, NAUTILUS, OSTRICH, OWL, PANTHER, PEACOCK, PENGUIN, PETREL, PLOVER, PYTHON, QUAIL, RAMBLER, RAVEN, SEAL, SWALLOW, SWIFT, VANGUARD.

52 butties: January 1949: AIRE, AMESBURY, AMY, AUSTRALIA, BASCOTE, DART, DAWLEY, DEE, DENMARK, DEVON, DILYS, DORSET, DRAYTON, ELSIE, ENA, EVENLODE, EXE, FANNY, FAY, FAZELEY, FLORENCE, FORWARD, FREDA, GERTIE, GLADYS, GLASGOW, GRANGE, GREET, GRETA, GRIMSBY, HARTFORD, HELEN, HETTIE, IDA, ITALY, IVER, JERSEY, JOAN, KESWICK, NATAL, PENKRIDGE, PRETORIA, ROMFORD, ROUMANIA, SPAIN, TRING, UPWOOD, UXBRIDGE,YARDLEY, YEADING, YIEWSLEY, YORK.

ERNEST THOMAS, WALSALL

42 boats: APOLLO (m) 05.46, BESSIE 01.42, BULBOURNE 01.42, CLARA 01.42, COUNT (m) 10.47, DIAMOND 06.44, DUTEOUS (m) 04.45, EGYPT 12.48, ENVOY (m) 02.48, GENERAL (m) 07.46, GOOLE 01.42, GOSPORT 08.48, GRANTHAM 04.45, JAMES 01.42, JAPAN 01.42, JUBILEE (m) 12.41, KEGWORTH 01.42, KERRY 08.48, KILBURN 07.48, KILDARE 08.48, KING (m) 07.47, KINGSBURY 04.45, LEIGHTON 04.41, LONGTON 04.45, MIDDLESEX 08.48, PILOT (m) 07.41, POLE STAR (m) 08.39, PRESIDENT (m) 06.46, ROSE 01.42, RUSSIA 08.48, SEAGULL (m) 12.45, SOMERSET 09.46, STANLEY 05.46, STONE 12.41, SUFFOLK 07.47, SULTAN (m) 12.41, SUSSEX 09.46, SWEDEN 08.48, VENUS 06.41, VICEROY (m) 08.48, VULCAN (m) 09.47, WINSFORD 06.46. *(In addition he is believed to have purchased the engines out of the bombed motors ROBIN and ROVER)*

UNION ACID COMPANY LIMITED, MANCHESTER

30 boats: ARROW 11.07, AYLESBURY 04.15, BLUEBELL 05.12, COLE 12.11, COWLEY 11.15, DAISY 03.06, DEE 12.14, DENHAM 01.15, DIGBY 06.24, DOVE 10.01, GEORGE 02.13, HANDSWORTH 02.00, LEICESTER 10.00, LEO 01.14, MOORE 02.18, PRIMROSE 01.14, ROSE IN JUNE 02.00, SAMUEL 02.10, SPONDON 10.15, STAR 10.99, STORT 12.04, SYDNEY 10.99, TAME 01.04, TEME 01.04, TORQUAY 05.98, TYNE 02.02, VIOLET 04.08, WALES 03.15, WEEDON 10.99, WINDSOR 10.08.

WILLIAM NURSER & SONS (later NURSER BROTHERS), BRAUNSTON

20 boats: BEECH 04.24, BLACKCOCK 05.29, CLENT 05.29, CREWE 05.29, DAFFODIL 09.12, EUTOCA 07.12, FIR 02.24, IRELAND 09.12, LARCH 02.24, LEMON 02.28, LUDLOW 05.12, MONMOUTH 07.27, NORTON 02.13, NORWOOD 05.15, OLTON 03.26, PIONEER 07.12, POPLAR 08.27, ROCHDALE 05.29, SCOTLAND 05.15, WEDNESBURY 05.15.

Belmont Publications - The 'Working Waterways' Series

This series gives wide circulation to the accounts of those who worked on England's waterways. The books form an authoritative record of a now vanished world – an invaluable source for waterways and social historians.

(All are A5 - Portrait, paperback)

1) Maidens' Trip by Emma Smith
2) Troubled Waters by Margaret Cornish
3) Bread upon the Waters by David Blagrove
4) Idle Women by Susan Woolfitt
5) The Amateur Boatwomen by Eily Gayford
6) Anderton for Orders by Tom Foxon - the first of the trilogy
7) Quiet Waters By by David Blagrove
8) Hold on a Minute by Tim Wilkinson
9) Number One by Tom Foxon - the second of the trilogy
10) Following the Trade by Tom Foxon - the last of the trilogy

Other titles, in this series, will follow

Other Belmont publications

Clothes of the Cut by Avril Lansdell (A4 landscape)
Colours for Cruisers by John Hill (A4 landscape)
From Stem to Stern by John Hill (A4 landscape)
Still Waters by Margaret Cornish (A5 portrait)
Walking on Water by Nick Corble (A5 portrait)

We specialise in Waterways Books